D0396200

HARNESSING THE INCREDIBLE POWER OF FEAR

Harnessing the Incredible Power of Fear

By Dr. Ken Nichols

Foreword by
Dr. David Jeremiah

Counseling Ministries

© 1996 by ALIVE Counseling Ministries
2100 Greenfield Dr.
El Cajon, CA 92019
All Rights Reserved

ISBN 1-885447-05-1

Published by Walk Thru the Bible Ministries, Atlanta, Georgia

Scripture quotations are taken from The Holy Bible, New
International Version, Copyright © 1973, 1987, 1984 International
Bible Society. Used by permission of Zondervan Bible Publishers.

DEDICATION

Marlene, my lovely wife of 30 years (8/27/66), without a doubt has been a consistent source of encouragement and strength. She also has been my personal secretary during the past 10 years. Her timely words of encouragement, her patience with the time investment this project required and her reminders that God will impact lives through it, kept me writing and rewriting.

I also want to express my deep gratitude and love to my wonderful parents who provided a solid foundation, who taught by example, whose love for God and family is contagious and whose faithful prayer support is at the core of God's blessing on our lives and ministry.

CONTENTS

Fear Can Motivate Us
Destructive Fear Will Manipulate Us
A. Fear Can Cause Cowardice
B. Fear Often Creates Confusion
C. Confusion Can Cause Fear
D. Fear Can Eventually Control Us

Fear Causes Us to Think Irrationally
Fear Invites Us to Rationalize
Fear Casts Doubt on God's Forgiveness
Fear Creates the Illusion of Perfection
Fear Compels Us to Expect the Worst

Fear Interacts With Worry and Anxiety
Fear Inflames Anger
Fear Invites Depression

Fear and Your Heart
Fear and Cancer
Fear and Your Immune System
Fear and Pain
Fear and Recovery from Illness
Fear and Death

ACKNOWLEDGEMENTS

Accepting a new and unfamiliar challenge can be invigorating as well as exhausting. The decision to write this book was primarily a result of much encouragement from my pastor and friend David Jeremiah. His commitment to excellence, passion for ministry and genuine enthusiasm for writing are contagious.

Many have contributed financially to make this project possible. Joe and Cathy Zehr have provided consistent and generous support to Alive Ministries and have taken special interest in this book project. I am deeply grateful.

Several family members and friends were willing to read and re-read the manuscript in its developing stages.

Ron Barnes gave direction and practical help with Bible content.

Carol Lacy provided faithful, professional, editorial assistance with a gracious and patient spirit. Her capable influence is evident from cover to cover. She was a good encourager.

Thank you, all.

ABOUT THE AUTHOR

Dr. Ken Nichols is currently the Vice President of Student Development at Christian Heritage College in El Cajon, California. He also serves on the Senior Staff of the Shadow Mountain Community Church as Pastor of Family Ministries.

Dr. Nichols graduated from Cedarville College, earned a masters degree from Wright State University followed by a second masters and doctorate degree from Rosemead Graduate School of Psychology, Biola University in 1979.

He founded ALIVE Counseling Ministries in 1979 while on the staff of the Blackhawk Baptist Church in Fort Wayne, Indiana. ALIVE Ministries is a Christian non-profit corporation providing seminars by Dr. Nichols in locations around the country. Seminars are available on cassette tape.

Dr. Nichols and his wife Marlene were married in 1966 and have three children: Mark, Kendra and Kara. Additions to the family include their son-in-law, Brad Soucie and daughter-in-law, Kristy (Tolmie) and most recently a granddaughter, Savannah Joy. Ken and Marlene have been involved in full-time ministry during their 30 years of marriage.

ALIVE COUNSELING MINISTRIES

Alive Ministries is a multi-faceted, church-oriented approach to the counseling needs of the Christian community. ALIVE, which stands for **A**lways **L**iving **I**n **V**iew of **E**ternity, is dedicated to helping others and training others to help.

SEMINAR SERIES

Dr. Nichols has developed 11 topical seminars that are available in four-cassette albums. The topics were developed in response to the counseling agendas of the many hundreds of people he has ministered to over the last 25 years. The titles of these seminars are as follows:

1. Age-Old Truth for New Age Times
2. The Master's Blueprint for Managing Burdens
3. Dealing with the Dangers of Discontent
4. Release from the Bondage of Fears through the Building of Faith
5. Dynamic Principles for Partnership
6. Prescription for a Healthy Heart
7. Portrait of a Person from a Biblical Perspective

SEMINAR SERIES
(Continued)

El Temor

A Spanish version of this book is available in condensed form. Several thousand copies have been circulated in South America to help Christians in their daily lives. To order please call 619-590-1747 or send your request to:

ALIVE Counseling Ministries
2100 Greenfield Dr.
El Cajon, CA 92019

FORWARD
by David Jeremiah

To live is to face fear. Sometimes there is valid reason for it. On other occasions we are just caught by surprise. Sometimes our fears are imagined and not real. But the effect upon our system is usually the same whether there is any basis for our fear or not.

In my twenty-five years as a Pastor-teacher, I have encountered many varieties of fear. I have been with families as some tragic news is communicated and watched fear paralyze. I have been in the hospital room when the doctor has told his patient that the illness is serious and perhaps life-threatening. I have counseled parents whose children have run away! I have tried to help spouses who have just been told that their partner has unexpectedly filed for divorce! I have been present when a doctor has told two young parents that something is wrong with their newborn.

I have stood in front of large crowds to speak and have been personally filled with fear. I have been stabbed to the heart with fear as I have seen my sons take vicious hits on the football field and then just lay there for what seemed like hours. I stayed all night with my daughter Jennifer in the hospital room after she had been injured in a soccer game and suffered a severe concussion. I have watched as my own children entered a new classroom situation for the first time! I have prayed as I dropped my high school graduates off at a far away college for further education and sensed the twinge of fear that says, "What if I don't fit in here . . . What if I'm not accepted?"

I have also personally known the kind of fear that grips one's whole system when he is told that he has a serious disease. Fear is not a stranger to me and probably not to you either. You picked up this book because it resonated with something you have experienced personally or shared deeply with another. If we're honest we're all a lot like the little boy who had a part in the school play that read, "It is I; be not afraid." He came out on stage and said, "It's me and I'm scared."

What about Christians and fear? Should we ever fear? Can fear ever be conquered? What do we say to those we know who are being crippled by this emotion? Can fear really be harnessed into something productive and good? The answers to many of these questions are in your hands in this new book by my friend, Dr. Ken Nichols. With a conviction born out of many hours of study and personal counseling, he challenges us to turn our fear into faith! He dares us to take something threatening and turn it into something thrilling!

For over twenty years I have worked alongside Dr. Nichols and have observed his deep love for the Word of God and for the people of God. Often we have shared together the joy of devoting our lives to the eternal Word of God and the eternal souls of men!

In many respects, my job is not as difficult as his. I study the Word and then teach it, usually to very large groups. I trust God to use His Word to change lives. Sometimes I find out what He has done. Most of the time I am left to trust the promise that His Word will not return unto Him void but will accomplish that unto which He sent it! I believe that promise and have learned to rest my case there.

But counseling is different. Thrown into life-struggles of men and women, one or two at a time, can be far more draining! When my listeners fail to really listen and choose to do nothing with my Biblical counsel, I usually do not hear about it unless it results in some major failure. But Biblical Counselors

have to face the weekly realities of unfollowed
instructions and ignored advice. Frankly, I do not
know how they survive. I am confident that it is not
my gift! But it truly is Dr. Ken Nichols' gift. He consistently applies the truth of God's Word to the human
problems of our day and prayerfully, patiently waits
for God to work.

And God has worked! I could tell you the stories
of many marriages that have been saved and many
human souls that have been mended. Ken would be
quick to say that God did it and he is correct. But
perhaps you have noticed that God does some of His
best work through yielded servants. I have appreciat-
ed and benefited from Ken Nichols' encouragement
and wisdom and for years I have encouraged Ken to
put his seminar material in writing. I teased and
bugged him until he got the message and now you
will get the message too.

INTRODUCTION

My wife Marlene and I were spending a weekend away for rest and enjoyment. Our daughter Kendra and her husband Brad joined us in a lovely hotel on the bay in San Diego, ideal for a relaxing overnight retreat. In just a split second fear became an uninvited fifth guest of our holiday when we were awakened at 4:34 A.M. by noise and the shaking of our bed. Earthquake! Marlene jumped out of bed and had her jogging suit and shoes on in just a few seconds. We were on the fourteenth floor (not a good place to be during an earthquake), and the building was still swaying back and forth. Hotel guests struggled with their fear encounter. Some screamed, some ducked for cover, and others ran out of their rooms, trying to get out of the building.

Even though none of the hotel guests was injured we all experienced a full range of unharnessed fear and seeming helplessness. Almost 40 minutes later, after getting TV reports of death and destruction in and around Northridge, we settled down enough to get back in bed. Suddenly the voice of the hotel manager came over the speaker. Marlene and I jumped up again. An aftershock? He announced that engineers had checked the building's foundation, that we had no cause to fear and should try to get back to sleep. Right! Later that morning we found out that the hotel was constructed with the latest state-of-the-art technology. It was mounted on rollers, which accounted for the terrifying swaying.

The Northridge earthquake on January 17, 1994 killed 55 people. Structural damage was estimated to be in the multiple millions of dollars.

But much more complicated than rebuilding the devastated buildings and highways of a sprawling city is the slow and cautious process of rebuilding human emotional balance. Recovery from the devastating effects of unharnessed fear is often a painful and gradual process.

Emotional Manipulation

It is not possible to calculate or even estimate the initial emotional damage and ongoing invasion of fear into every area of life following such terrifying experiences. Feeling the "solid" earth beneath you come alive, twisting as if something were trying to escape from its core, is so very frightening. Many families refused to go back into their homes, camping instead in cars or in city parks. For them, fear had not been harnessed and its power was free to dominate their lives.

Some office workers even wore hard hats to work for several days after the initial quake! Many families packed their belongings—or what was left of them—and left California, not having the strength or knowledge to harness the powerful emotion of fear. Thousands of aftershocks of that disastrous quake have been recorded and still continue at this writing. People in the Los Angeles area are being bombarded by fear. The sounds of a low-flying jet spurs momentary panic. A semi-truck rumbling by triggers the fearful reaction "EARTHQUAKE!" Each aftershock increases pulse rates, produces tears, causes clammy palms, and sends school children and workers in high-rise buildings under desks and doorways.

Since then there have been even more devastating quakes in Kobe, Japan, and in an oil town on Sakhalin Island in Russia. All over our globe floods, tornadoes, and further quakes seem to be trying to tear our earth apart. Not only is our world being pounded by natural disasters, but both Japan and the U.S. have, for the first time, been subjected to frightening terrorist attacks. Imagine getting on the subway every day knowing, as do the people of Japan, that you might be caught in a poison gas attack. Residents of Oklahoma City—and indeed the entire nation—will continue to feel the aftermath of fear caused by the terrorist bombing of the federal building. These fear-saturated incidents, and many others ranging from the common to the unique, reflect the central focus of this book.

My daughter Kendra related that her first reaction during the earthquake was to cry out to God for protection. But no one, Christian or non-Christian, can be insulated from the reality of natural and man-caused disasters that spontaneously generate feelings of fear and, for many, terrible loss. Even the most spiritual person finds they are unable to avoid confrontation with this powerful emotion.

Our hearts are routinely gripped by fear as we experience, read about, or view fear-producing situations graphically portrayed on our television screens. Not everyone will face such dramatic fears as hanging by the fingertips from a roof-top several stories above heavy traffic. But many will be damaged emotionally and spiritually as they become entangled in unharnessed fears, both real and imagined.

Fear-generating events, whether the concrete kind that dramatically disrupt your life, or the more subtle, abstract, often imaginary ones that can become a chronic life-style, will accompany us all our lives. The critical question is not, "Will I be afraid?" but rather, "How will I manage the fears that I will surely face?"

The good news and the primary message of this book is that we can learn to harness the awesome power of fear so it does not control our view of ourselves, our relationship with other people, and our fellowship with God.

Spiritual Warfare

It is very important to understand that the battle with fear goes beyond the emotional arena. Struggling with fear is fundamentally and primarily a spiritual battle. "For our struggle is not against flesh and blood, but against the rulers, against the authorities, against the powers of this dark world and against the spiritual forces of evil in the heavenly realms" (Ephesians 6:12).

All of life is a battleground, a spiritual struggle with God and those who pledge their allegiance to Him on one side, and Satan and his myriad subjects on the other. The Apostle Peter both warned and instructed us about this spiritual battle: "Be self-controlled and alert. Your enemy the devil prowls around like a roaring lion looking for someone to devour. Resist him, standing firm in the faith" (1 Peter 5:8-9). One calculating, effective strategy of that "roaring lion" is to exhaust us emotionally, physically, and spiritually with chronic, unharnessed fear. Then, when we are totally fatigued by that fear he can impose his evil schemes with laser-sharp accuracy. Ultimate success in warfare requires that we know the strength and strategy of the Enemy, in order, as Paul said, "that Satan might not outwit us." For we cannot afford to be "unaware of his schemes" (2 Corinthians 2:11).

Along with warfare intelligence we need weapons to defend ourselves, and spiritual warfare requires spiritual weapons. A soldier would never be sent into combat without instruction and training on how to use his weapons. It is the same for Christians; we can defend ourselves against the destructive power of our spiritual Adversary if we know ahead of time what weapons he will use and how we, through supernatural resources, can neutralize those weapons. We must equip ourselves to resist our Enemy, the Evil One, in all areas of our lives, including harnessing fear, if we are to avoid becoming a casualty of spiritual warfare.

This book is a spiritual warfare intelligence report, so to speak, on how you can be spiritually equipped to do battle in a fear-dominated warfare. Four main sections of the book identify important questions about fear. The first section addresses the SIGNIFICANCE OF FEAR and answers the question: "What is fear?" The second section, the SYMPTOMS OF FEAR, deals with the question: "How does fear manifest itself in my life?" The third section identifies the primary SOURCES OF FEAR by asking, "What aspects of my nature are at the core of most of my fears?" Answers to these important questions will equip you to apply, faithfully and effectively, Biblically-sound and lasting SOLUTIONS TO UNHARNESSED FEARS as you journey from living in fear to living by faith. These solutions are covered in the fourth section, which answers the question, "How can I not only keep away from fear's bondage but learn to harness the great and the small fears of life?"

Fear that is not supernaturally harnessed will pursue us relentlessly. Unharnessed fear will chase us until we are exhausted, weak, and ready to quit. The following story from Kay Arthur's book *To Know Him By Name* captures the essence of what this book is all about.

> My friend tells the story of something that happened while his dad was deer hunting in the wilds of Oregon.
>
> Cradling his rifle in the crook of his arm, his dad was following an old logging road nearly overgrown by the encroaching forest. It was early evening, and he was just thinking about returning to camp when a noise exploded in the brush nearby. Before he even had a chance to lift his rifle, a small blur of brown and white came shooting up the road straight for him.
>
> My friend laughs as he tells the story.

"It all happened so fast, Dad hardly had time to think. He looked down and there was a little brown cottontail—utterly spent—crowded up against his legs between his boots. The little thing was trembling all over; but it just sat there and didn't budge.

"Now this was really strange. Wild rabbits are frightened of people, and it's not that often that you'd ever actually see one—let alone have one come and sit at your feet.

"While Dad was puzzling over this, another player entered the scene. Down the road—maybe twenty yards away—a weasel burst out of the brush. When it saw my dad—and its intended prey sitting at his feet—the predator froze in its tracks, its mouth panting, its eyes glowing red.

"It was then Dad understood he had stepped into a little life-and-death drama of the forest. The cottontail, exhausted by the chase, was only moments from death. Dad was its last hope of refuge. Forgetting its natural fear and caution, the little animal instinctively crowded up against him for protection from the sharp teeth of its relentless enemy.

"My friend's father did not disappoint. He raised his powerful rifle and deliberately shot into the ground just underneath the weasel. The animal seemed to leap almost straight into the air a couple of feet and then rocketed back into the forest as fast as its legs could move.

"For a while, the little rabbit didn't stir. It just sat there, huddled at the man's feet in the gathering twilight while he spoke gently to it.

"'Where did he go, little one? I don't think he'll be bothering you for a while. Looks like you're off the hook tonight.' Soon the rabbit hopped away from its protector into the forest."

Where, Beloved, do you run in time of need?

Where do you run when the predators of trouble, worry, and fear pursue you?

Where do you hide when your past pursues you like a relentless wolf, seeking your destruction?

Where do you seek protection when the weasels of temptation, corruption, and evil threaten to overtake you?

Where do you turn when your energy is spent . . . when weakness saps you and you feel you cannot run away any longer?

Do you turn to your protector, the One who stands with arms open wide, waiting for you to come and huddle in the security of all He is? [1]

We too, ultimately must hasten to the Saviour's feet, perhaps trembling with exhaustion and fear, but somehow knowing that His strength, His power, His protection will keep us from being consumed by the incredible power of fear.

Note:
[1] Arthur, Kay. *To Know Him By Name*. Sisters, Oregon: Multnomah Books, 1995: 5-6.

SECTION
ONE

THE
SIGNIFICANCE
OF FEAR

chapter

What is Fear?
Friend or Foe?

According to the National Institute of Health, 24 million Americans suffer from feelings of fear intense enough to interfere with their daily routines. Twenty-four million—the total populations of Los Angeles, New York City, Chicago, and Dallas. The loss of productivity and effectiveness due to fear is inestimable. Fear comes in many guises; perhaps the most common type of controlling fear is the phobia.

A phobia is "an anxiety disorder characterized by an obsessive, irrational, and intense fear." [1] Some of the better-known phobias are:

Agoraphobia—fear of open places
Claustrophobia—fear of being trapped
Laliophobia—fear of talking
Nyctophobia—fear of the dark
Xenophobia—fear of strangers
Zoophobia—fear of animals

If you've experienced one or more of these phobias, I'm sure you would not consider it "irrational." To you, there's nothing irrational about being afraid of getting trapped, even if it is being trapped in a gigantic traffic jam in a parking lot after a football game. And, sure, a lot of people have a morbid fear of public speaking, and they don't consider it irrational when their knees knock together like cymbals in a pep band. Also, don't we encourage our children to be afraid of strangers? Surely, that's not irrational. And anyone who doesn't steer clear of a snarling, barking dog isn't rational. Phobias are fears that have become magnified and exaggerated in the mind of the person experiencing them, so that he is no longer able to function normally because of them.

Phobias or magnified fears, however, are not the only kinds of fears we face. *The unknown creates fear.* Over the last decade our attention has been dominated by such fear-inducing issues as co-dependency, dysfunctional families, addictive personalities, abuse, healing of memories, false memories and a host of others. Sensationalized media attention to these subjects caused many to become excessively preoccupied with their own dysfunctional pasts, creating a perfect atmosphere for a variety of fears to flourish.

Preoccupation with the past creates fear. Even though many thousands of people have not come from a classic dysfunctional family, exaggerated attention to such life issues can cause them to be preoccupied with the past. It is so easy to transfer from a legitimate concern to a controlling obsession. Looking back is reasonable. Living there can result in being saturated with fear.

Paranoia about the future creates fear. Of equal concern is an obsession with the future which creates an ideal environment for fear to grow. We can spend exorbitant amounts of emotional and physical energy feeling paranoid about the future—world economy, shaky political alliances, terrorism, crime, broken relationships, drugs, disease, natural disasters. Thus the bomb shelter business flourished in the 60's. Now, in the 90's, Christine Gorman observes that paranoia is still a gradual descent—beginning with a slight, a hurt, a grievance. When these feelings are focused on and nurtured with fear, the paranoia that spawns terrorism has begun.[2] Fear-drenched preoccupation with the past and paranoia about the future cause paralysis in the present. You can count on it. What a powerful and clever strategy of the Adversary. And believe me, it really works.

The emotion of fear need not be sinful or harmful. Fear is not the problem; it is whether we harness it or it harnesses us. Fear that is harnessed can become a powerful motivator and constructive energy source.

Fear Can Motivate Us

Motivating fear is good; it is part of the emotional equipment given to us at birth—even before birth, for babies in the womb have been known to jump at loud noises. Many fears are positive and productive because they prod us to do something about the fearful situation. Natural, God-given, motivating fear protects us from dangers that lurk in the shadows; hazards that exist as a result of a sin-cursed world; things that could do us personal harm. It is what comes into play when you step off the curb, hear a loud honk and jump back just as a car screeches by. For the next few minutes your heart pounds and pulse races. But you soon relax. The danger has passed and motivating fear has rescued you from harm.

The watchful care of motivating fear keeps you from touching a hot stove, walking too near a cliff edge, or turning the wrong way on a one-way street. In moments of danger, motivating fear activates your sense of self-preservation and survival as it pumps adrenaline into your bloodstream, allowing you to face impending danger with courage and confidence. Motivating fear causes a husband to walk five days in the snow to get help for his stranded family or a young mother to find strength to lift a car off her toddler. In these ways the harnessed power of fear is our friend.

Throughout life we face circumstances that will generate fear. However, we often find ourselves at a crossroad: one road leads to a productive, motivating fear, the other to negative, manipulative fear. We do have the freedom to choose which direction we will pursue.

It is important to understand that a very thin line separates motivating and manipulating fear. In fact, the emotion of fear is dynamic and spontaneous, and often what starts out as motivating fear (the commitment to do something about the fear-causing situation) turns into manipulating fear (a form of emotional paralysis). It is as though the energy reserves which God intended for EMERGENCY USE ONLY leak out little by little in our battles with fear, leaving us emotionally paralyzed and spiritually exhausted. This is what happened with some fishermen on the Sea of Galilee.

No seasoned fisherman would ever get caught on the Sea of Galilee in a storm of great intensity. Yet, Jesus' disciples—several of them experienced fishermen—found themselves battling the furies of the worst tempest they had ever known. The little boats were being tossed about like corks on a white-water river.

Motivating fear had led them to do all they could to save the valuable fishing boats and their own lives. They had turned the boats into the wind, furiously bailed out water, tossed overboard any fish or other cargo they carried. But when all their human efforts were exhausted, they still faced an utterly hopeless and helpless situation (Mark 4:35-41).

The furor of the storm so dominated their hearts that they held little hope of outlasting the angry waves and roaring wind. But wait! Jesus was in the stern of one of the boats, asleep on a cushion. The disciples, possibly resenting His peaceful nap, thinking that He didn't care that they were about to drown, woke Him. Jesus got up and with only a few words told the wild, convulsive sea to be still. Immediately the sea was tamed. After He rebuked the sea Jesus turned and rebuked His disciples, "Why are you so afraid? Do you still have no faith?" (Mark 4:40), as if to say, "Did you allow your fear to manipulate you, even to the point of forgetting that I was with you?" The disciples' faith in the miracle-working Jesus had been distracted by fear, leaving a vacuum into which controlling, manipulating fear poured. (We will develop the relationship between fear and faith in a later chapter.)

Without a doubt many thousands of people facing fearful circumstances have been overwhelmed by the power of unharnessed fear that spoiled their joy and purpose in life.

I will never forget my first meeting and interview with someone who was being manipulated by a variety of fears and powerful anxieties. Janet's exaggerated fears were immediately apparent as soon as I saw her in the waiting room. Even though she was already taking prescribed anti-anxiety medication, it was incredibly obvious in her countenance that she was on the threshold of a major anxiety attack.

Janet's life illustrated how powerful manipulative fear can be. By the time she was referred for counseling, her fear and anxiety had resulted in her leaving her job, losing communication with her family, and feeling far from God. Janet's experience illustrates how powerful manipulative fear can become.

Destructive Fear Will Manipulate Us

You may not struggle with fear at the same level as Janet, but I am sure you will be able to identify certain aspects of fear that can disrupt your life. Fear can cause you to become cowardly; fear can cause you to be confused, just as confusion can cause fear. Unharnessed fear will eventually control you.

Fear can cause cowardice. Fear that produces cowards is a powerful weapon in any kind of warfare. Psychological warfare, media communication, leaflets dropped in battle zones, organized anti-war demonstrations—all intended to break the enemy's resolve and create more intense fear—have always been an essential part of successful war strategy. The former USSR invested millions to develop a "fear gas" that could not be resisted by will or normal bravery but was designed to create fear and rob their enemies of the courage to fight. Not so long ago, newspaper headlines showed relentless media posturing by the United States designed to intimidate rebel generals in Haiti. There were repeated scenes of special task force meetings, warships on the move, and the tiny country being covered with leaflets promising to use military force, if necessary, to restore the exiled leader and a future hope for democracy. The purpose of these tactics was to create a loss of resolve by cultivating a cowardly response.

The consequences of cowardly fear are graphically depicted in a familiar Bible story recorded in the book of Numbers. Under Moses' leadership, the people of God were finally coming to the end of their journey from Egypt to their homeland. While the people stood on the threshold of their destination, the land which God had promised them, God told Moses to send out twelve men, one from each tribe, to spy out the land ahead so that Moses would know what his competition was like. After 40 days of spying, the 12 men returned, bearing pomegranates and figs, and a single cluster of grapes so heavy that it had to be carried by two men. The spies proclaimed that the land surely flowed with milk and honey. But ten of the 12 gave a cowardly report: "We can't attack those people; they are stronger than we are. . . . The land we explored devours those living in it. . . . All the people we saw there are of great size. We seemed like grasshoppers in our own eyes, and we looked the same to them" (Numbers 13:31-33). They were truly intimidated by the awesome giants.

Only two of the spies gave a courageous report and believed that the land could be taken with the help of the all-powerful Most High God. But the people sided with the ten. They were afraid of the giants. Their cowardly fear had great, long-term consequences. Because of their lack of faith, none of that generation entered the Promised Land except the two men who conquered cowardly, intimidating fear by seeing the land with all of its fear-generating challenges through the eyes of faith.

Not only does cowardly fear threaten our physical courage, as the giants in the Promised Land threatened the spies, but our spiritual enemy, Satan, is highly skilled at turning us into cowards as we face routine battles of Christian living, making them appear as "giants." Giant look-a-likes, creating a cowardly response, can turn you into a chronic coward, propagating "low-risk" and "no-risk" living. Shrinking from danger and running from fearful situations can evolve from one trivial, isolated incident to a habit you excuse as only a personal quirk. Undetected and unchallenged, this cowardly lifestyle will complicate your life and contribute to eternal losses.

People subject to cowardly fear are afraid of rejection, so they avoid risk in business ventures; they hesitate to propose new ideas; they shun responsibility. Their lives are dedicated to placating feelings of fear. They prefer to make a deal: "I promise to take no risks if manipulative fear will just leave me alone."

It is not possible to estimate the losses which cowardly fear can cause in our lives. We would all benefit from doing a sincere damage assessment in this area of spiritual warfare. The Book of Hebrews tells the stories of men and women who faced awful, fear-causing situations but were still able to overcome the temptation to cowardly retreat. In addition, many missionaries have faced enormous fears that stood in the way of reaching villages for Christ. As God enabled them to overcome their fear, they were wonderfully rewarded with an entire tribe coming to know Christ. But also true are the many stories of Christians faced with such fears that kept them from serving in their local churches or even from becoming missionaries.

Sandy stopped in New York on her way to Ethiopia for a mission term when she met Carl. Because she feared living life as a single, Sandy decided to cancel her trip just to see what would come of this relationship. She married Carl, an unbeliever. Years later she looked back and said, "I often wonder what my life would be if I had followed God's call." Are there issues in your life in which you are being manipulated by a fear-induced cowardly lifestyle? Remember that "you did not receive [an evil] spirit that makes you a slave again to fear, but you received the [Holy] Spirit of sonship" (Romans 8:15). You can and should be free from the power of cowardly fear!

Fear often creates confusion. A second way that fear manipulates us is by interacting with the unknown, creating fear-related confusion. Confusion can invoke fear, and fear can cause further confusion. Confusion reflects a spontaneous and temporary emotional response to a frightening situation. Unexpected events, alarming news, sudden noises, or even the unexpected ring of the telephone can trigger fear-related confusion and disorientation that may last for seconds or, depending on the nature of the call, for months.

A young mother answers the door. A policeman standing there begins, "I'm sorry, there's been an accident." Her mind clouds and blocks the rest of the message. "How can this be? . . . what happened? . . . it's a mistake . . . what must I do? . . . this isn't true." Total confusion! All this before she finds out the extent of the accident, which may not be as devastating as she imagines.

A middle-aged man sits in the examining room. The doctor apologetically begins, "I'm sorry, it's malignant." The man's mind races: "What do you mean 'malignant'? . . . I don't have time for this . . . am I going to die? . . . what about my family? . . . what about my job?" And it takes a few days for the fear-driven confusion to subside enough for him to think rationally about his treatment options.

Confusion can cause fear. God knows how fear can cause confusion, and the ensuing confusion can generate more fear. He used this kind of fear against the enemies of His people. He promised Moses and the Hebrew people that in their journey across the wilderness, "I will send my terror ahead of you and throw into confusion every nation you encounter. I will make all your enemies turn their backs and run" (Exodus 23:27).

Later, God used confusion to rout one of their enemies, the Midianites. A fraction of the Hebrew army, only 300 men led by Gideon, was sent by God carrying not weapons of war, but trumpets and clay jars hiding lit torches. Instead of attacking with swords and spears, the soldiers surrounded the enemy camp, blew trumpets, broke the clay jars uncovering hundreds of flickering torches, and shouted, "A sword for the LORD and for Gideon!" The result? "All the Midianites ran, crying out as they fled . . . the LORD caused the men throughout the camp to turn on each other with their swords"

(Judges 7:21-22). Confusing fear led to a grievous and embarrassing defeat. That night's campfire conversation among the Midianite soldiers who escaped death must have gone something like this, "You've got to be kidding! Three hundred unarmed men put all the glory of our military machine in shambles?"

And of course we all know that any strategy God chooses to use for His purposes the Adversary attempts to duplicate for his destructive work. He has mastered the art of creating fear-related confusion as a means to distract us from God's clear truth and an honest, reality-based assessment of the frightening circumstances we face. The less we understand the circumstances we are dealing with, the greater the potential for fear to work its way into our hearts. Confusion-related fear can cause inaction, inappropriate action, and an ineffective waste of energy. Confusing fear has the power to defeat us, even spiritually.

Fear can eventually control us. This third kind of manipulative fear, fear that can take control of your life, is by far the most damaging because it requires all your attention, energy, and obedience. Drivers of lumber-laden semi-trucks in the Colorado mountains are protected from a kind of fear that could control them to the extent that their driving would be impaired. This protection is in the form of sand-filled safety ramps constructed alongside downhill roads. As long as the brakes hold on these heavy trucks, the driver can competently and safely keep his truck on the road as it whizzes along. However, if the brakes go, the driver is simply along for the ride, hurtling down the mountain road until he can direct his vehicle onto one of the ramps. When controlled, the truck is a tool for productive service. When controlling, it turns into an implement of potential destruction. So is the case with the incredible power of fear that is not harnessed. We need to find "safety ramps" in life that will protect us from being controlled by fear.

King Saul had a major confrontation with fear when he met Goliath. When the giant Philistine challenged Israel, "Saul," and indeed, "all the Israelites were dismayed and terrified" (1 Samuel 17:11). A young shepherd boy stepped forward with only a slingshot and shouted at the giant, "In the name of the LORD Almighty . . . I'll strike you down and cut off your head" (v. 45-46). Shortly after David's stone felled the giant, Saul once again showed how fear so controlled him that it led him to try to "pin David to the wall" with a spear. "Saul was afraid of David, because the Lord was with David but had left Saul" (1 Samuel 18:12).

These initial fears began to grow within Saul and control him until, eventually, the threats of the Philistine army, the army God had told him He would defeat, caused Saul to be "afraid; terror filled his heart" (1 Samuel 28:5).

The final outcome of controlling fear for King Saul was when he actually got a witch to call Samuel back from the grave to inquire about his destiny. When Samuel revealed Saul's immediate future, the king "fell full length on the ground, filled with fear because of Samuel's words. His strength was gone" (1 Samuel 28: 20). Saul had become a slave of fear. In fact, during his last days on earth he was totally consumed with a vicious, ever-present fear that dominated his every thought.

Total worship demonstrates our relationship to our God and includes unconditional obedience. Saul's inability to harness the power of fear resulted in unconditional obedience. Fear became his god; he gave over rule of his life to fear. If we choose to obey the demands of controlling fear instead of Jehovah God's guidance, fear becomes our master and we submit to its demands.

A story in the *Los Angeles Times Magazine* gives a

contemporary illustration that parallels Saul's journey from the heights of fame and acclaim to a hopeless despair that ended in suicide. "March 13, 1990, Bruno Bettelheim [an internationally famous psychologist] was found dead on the floor of his new apartment in a Maryland nursing home, a plastic bag over his head and barbiturates in his bloodstream. The news of his death stunned the psychological community. For 50 years, Bruno Bettelheim had been acknowledged as one of the most important thinkers and practitioners in the field of psychology and child development."[3] Dr. Bettelheim was especially noted for helping people find hope where others saw only despair. The reported reason for his suicide? Fear had dominated his spirit. He took his own life because of fear of suffering and fear of living a purposeless life.

There are 366 "fear-nots" in the Bible. They do not suggest the absence of the emotion of fear; that is not humanly possible. Most are specific reminders of God's faithfulness or are invitations and opportunities for us to increase our faith. At the end of each chapter of this book are several fear-not verses on which you can prayerfully meditate when you are confronted with the various types of fear.

As you will see, the purpose of the fear-nots is not to give you complete freedom from every type of fear. That would be a disaster of sorts. Our goal is to help you learn how to master fear, to bring it into control, to harness it as a wind-surfer harnesses the power of the winds, or as one harnesses an unruly horse, to restrain it so that, like a rampaging river that engineers have dammed up, you make it your servant rather than your master. Therefore my friend, determine that the words FEAR NOT will provide a refreshing sense of personal purpose and partnership with Christ in your spiritual journey.

PERSONAL EVALUATION

1. How does fear in my life interfere with my advancement at work? (Perhaps I could make better progress in my chosen profession if I were not afraid to go back to school or to apply for the new position that just opened up.)

2. In what way does fear limit my closeness and vulnerability with significant others? (Perhaps I long for a closer relationship but am afraid to be vulnerable to pain or rejection or changes indigenous to developing relationships.)

3. In what way does fear limit my spiritual growth? (For example, am I afraid of being ridiculed for my faith? Or do I fear to take a stand against certain political/social issues that are clearly contrary to God's will because I may be called prejudiced or narrow-minded? Or perhaps my fear keeps me from making a commitment to teaching or serving in other ways.)

PRACTICAL APPLICATION

1. Read the psalm printed below, Psalm 91, every day for a week. Post a copy on your refrigerator, on your bed stand, or in your car. Believe that God has not changed. He will guard you just as He did the psalmist.

2. Write down a description of a fear you may be dealing with; label it cowardly, confusing, or controlling. Begin to think how you can defeat this fear by understanding it, praying about it, and believing God can force it out of control as you surrender that problem area of your life to Him.

3. Memorize 2 Timothy 1:7: "For God did not give us a spirit of timidity, but a spirit of power, of love and of self-discipline." Strive for this balance of power, love, and self-discipline in areas in your life that need to change and grow.

PRAYERFUL MEDITATION

*He who dwells in the shelter of the Most High will
rest in the shadow of the Almighty.
I will say of the LORD, "He is my refuge and my
fortress, my God, in whom I trust."
Surely he will save you from the fowler's snare
and from the deadly pestilence.
He will cover you with his feathers, and under his
wings you will find refuge; his faithfulness will be
your shield and rampart.
You will not fear the terror of night, nor the arrow
that flies by day,
nor the pestilence that stalks in the darkness, nor the
plague that destroys at midday.
A thousand may fall at your side,ten thousand at
your right hand, but it will not come near you.
You will only observe with your eyes and see the
punishment of the wicked.
If you make the Most High your dwelling—even the
LORD, who is my refuge—
then no harm will befall you, no disaster will come
near your tent.
For he will command his angels concerning you to
guard you in all your ways;
they will lift you up in their hands, so that you will
not strike your foot against a stone.
You will tread upon the lion and the cobra; you will
trample the great lion and the serpent.
"Because he loves me," says the LORD, "I will rescue
him; I will protect him, for he acknowledges my
name.
He will call upon me, and I will answer him; I will
be with him in trouble, I will deliver him and
honor him.
With long life will I satisfy him and show him my
salvation" (Psalm 91).*

Notes:
[1] *Mosby's Medical and Nursing Dictionary,* 2nd edition.
[2] Gorman, Christine. "Psst! Calling All Paranoids." *Time,* 8 May 1995: 69.
[3] *Los Angeles Times,* Magazine Section, 27 January 1991: 17-35.

SECTION
TWO

THE
SYMPTOMS
OF FEAR

chapter

Fear Affects Our Thinking

Almost without exception in both the medical and counseling fields, people who seek treatment begin their journey toward health and recovery by providing a thorough description of the symptoms. For instance, we recognize that a scratchy throat, achy joints, and the onset of sneezing are symptoms of a cold or the flu. Most physical illnesses give an early warning that something is not right within our bodies, and physicians listen carefully to our description of the symptoms. In the case of the flu, taking aspirin and antihistamines may mask the symptoms and help us feel better, but they won't cure the flu. Treatment requires that we pop vitamins, gulp orange juice, get extra rest, and maybe visit the doctor for antibiotics.

It is the same in counseling with people who have problems in their marriages, emotions, thinking, or behavior. Almost without exception, those who come for counseling, regardless of their problems, begin by giving a thorough description of their symptoms, how problems are affecting their lives. Successful treatment for the body and for personal problems is critically related to understanding the symptoms.

In this chapter we will survey various ways in which unharnessed fear manifests itself as specific symptoms in your thought life.

Unharnessed fear distorts thinking. The wise King Solomon said, "As [a person] thinks in his heart, so is he" (Proverbs 23:7, Amplified). What Solomon meant was that most of our actions and emotions are initiated in our thoughts. David the psalmist prayed, "Search me, O God, and know my heart; test me and know my anxious thoughts. See if there is any offensive way in me, and lead me in the way everlasting" (Psalm 139:23-24).

A personal experience shows how my distorted thinking was a classic symptom of unharnessed fear. I allowed unharnessed fear to run wild with my thinking when I received a registered letter from the Indiana State Board of Licensing one day. I was working in a church counseling ministry in Indiana as a state certified psychologist at the time. The letter read something like this:

Dear Dr. Nichols:

It has come to our attention that you may be in violation of rule number . . . and code number . . . of the Indiana Mental Health Professional Bureau. Individuals in violation of these statutes may receive fines, disciplinary action or the loss of license. Please be in contact with the State Board at your earliest convenience.

Upon reading the letter my heart began to race and it was almost impossible for me to focus my thoughts.

I reviewed the procedures we had followed in organizing the ALIVE Counseling Ministries. I was certain that we had carefully considered professional guidelines, but my mind began to create a "worst case scenario": I will be fined, lose my license, be subject to professional discipline and greatly embarrass the church, my family, and myself. What a tragedy! That night I couldn't sleep, was nauseated and had diarrhea. It was as though the power of fear came in without restraint and romped through my system. The endless "what-ifs" systematically paraded across the screen of my mind and imagination. Will this hit the local papers? What will my pastor and good friend David Jeremiah say? What about my professional colleagues in Fort Wayne? It was an absolutely fear-saturated night.

In the morning, exhausted and very much in the grip of manipulating fear, I began to develop a plan to harness my fears and clear up my distorted thinking. I called the State Board, and, with shaking hands, a dry throat, and a wimpy voice, I introduced myself and referred to the intimidating letter. When I had completed explaining our procedures I anxiously waited for his reply. Finally, after what seemed a lifetime, I heard, "Oops!" The person on the telephone casually explained that they had overlooked that we were a non-profit, religious organization, and affirmed that we had indeed established the ALIVE Counseling Ministries with appropriate professional guidelines.

My unharnessed fear had temporarily robbed me of the peace that is my right as one of God's family. I had to struggle to successfully manage the fear-generating situation in a mature way. For many hours I had been affected both emotionally and physically, suffering as if the worst had already happened. Looking back on this event I am embarrassed and a bit amused that the acronym for ALIVE Counseling

Ministries is Always Living In View of Eternity. Driven by unharnessed fear, all I could see was catastrophe. Becoming ALIVE again quieted the fears and cleared up my thinking.

Satan sends his fear into undisciplined, self-satisfied or formerly peaceful areas of our lives to keep us from correct, truthful, Biblical thinking. These looming terrors obscure our vision of God's truth so that our thoughts become dominated by the emotional reaction to the problem, and we fail to adhere to the facts of His promises. Fear of what others do, fear of retaliation, humiliation, failure, and God's judgment are all part of his arsenal, resulting in distorted thinking. In this way our Adversary not only prevents people from seeking salvation through Christ, he also blinds Christians to ways they can apply God's teachings to their lives, keeping them from realizing their full potential.

Fear Causes Us to Think Irrationally

To think irrationally means that our thoughts do not harmonize with reality. Interpreting a circumstance through fear can create an unreal scenario. Phobias, as reviewed earlier, are a good example of irrational thinking.

Fear-induced irrational thinking, in some cases called superstition, causes some people to check and recheck several times to see if the stove or iron has been turned off. One lady with such a concern would habitually, about ten minutes into their trip some-where, insist to her husband that she had left the iron on and the house would burn down. She would vehe-mently insist he turn the car around and go back home to check again. Understandably, it became a major source of irritation and conflict in their mar-riage. One time they were running a bit late for an appointment. As they reached the ten-minute mark, she grabbed her husband's arm and exclaimed,

"Honey, I left the iron on!" When he veered quickly into a gas station she was surprised and pleased that he didn't get upset, but was turning around to save the house from potential destruction. Instead, he stopped the car, removed the keys from the ignition, ran around to the rear of the car, popped the trunk, triumphantly lifted out the iron and handed it to his wife. Without another word they continued on to their destination. Her compromise with fear, bound up in unplugging the iron, was once again satisfied.

Fear Invites Us to Rationalize

Fear-induced rationalization is the second symptom to suggest that we are being manipulated by fear-distorted thinking. The finite mind, unprotected by God's supernatural truth, can rationalize and justify any decision. It just takes time. Rationalization means that we look at God's truth through eyes of self-sufficiency, and we will ultimately be tempted to bend the truth to deal with our fears.

Jeanette had been married for three years to Tom, but she was not happy. When she came for marital counseling she told how she had met Tom, how long they had dated, and how God had led in their decision to marry. And even though she described her husband as insensitive and selfish, she led me to believe that she wanted to pursue a Biblical plan for reconciliation and to establish a solid foundation for a lasting relationship. In my sessions with Tom he seemed highly motivated to save his marriage. However, when I met with the two of them together there was obvious tension and strong resistance on Jeanette's part.

In a private session Jeanette reluctantly began to tell me about a man, a fellow choir member, also married, who treated her with respect and thoughtfulness. She explained: "I feel more love, tenderness, and spiritual depth with him than I have ever experienced with my husband." Their relationship had grown over the months—including prayer together before each choir practice. After a year of phone calls, letters, and periodic private time together, they became emotionally committed and physically intimate. They both felt (rationalized) they had made a mistake in marrying their spouses and that God had led them together. They rationalized and justified their actions even though they knew that infidelity is prohibited by God.

Genuinely caring and committed Christians can rationalize and justify decisions in their lives that conflict with God's truth if they allow unharnessed fear to dominate them. Fearing that she would spend the rest of her life without being loved as she needed to be, Jeanette rationalized that God surely didn't want her to spend the rest of her life being miserable because she married the wrong man. She reasoned that God loves her and wants her to be happy. And happiness included being loved in a wonderful way by a man who met her need.

Her legitimate fears, which became exaggerated over time, resulted in a subtle and gradual fear-dominated distortion in her thinking. Her rationalization led to sinful, selfish decisions and, ultimately, to destructive consequences. She made a conscious choice not to conform her thoughts to God's truth and stand fast on the Word in the face of fear. What you believe influences how you behave.

Fear Casts Doubt On God's Forgiveness

Fear that can cause us to doubt that we are truly forgiven of our sins is another type of fear-induced distorted thinking. One of the most glorious promises in Scripture is found in John's first letter. No wonder then that the Adversary attacks this truth with such intensity. "If we confess our sins, he is faithful and just and will forgive us our sins and purify us from all unrighteousness" (1 John 1:9). Despite this great promise that God has forgiven their past sins, many Christians continue to suffer a controlling, doubt-induced fear.

Recognizing that we stand guilty before the right-eousness of God Most High first brings us to repentance and on to salvation through Jesus Christ who took the punishment for our sins. Recognizing that we are guilty of continuing in sin, falling short of the glory of God and grieving His loving, jealous heart plays a positive role in prodding us to walk in a manner worthy of our crucified and risen Savior. But when we nurture guilt until unbelief and fear dominate our lives, hamper our human relationships and block our fellowship with God, we give place to the Adversary.

Satan wins a battle in spiritual warfare if he can get us to question God's forgiveness which leads to disbelief in His promises. In spite of God's promise that "there is now no condemnation for those who are in Christ Jesus, because through Christ Jesus the law of the Spirit of life set me free from the law of sin and death" (Romans 8:1-2), many Christians live in fear because of their disbelief in God's forgiveness, and all the while the Deceiver throws back his head and laughs.

God forgives *all* our sin—past, present, and future. We no longer need to carry the guilt; Jesus paid for our sins on the cross. We must accept His gracious acquittal! We need to accept supernatural forgive-ness—unconditional, undeserved, and limitless in scope. When we are unwilling to believe God's offer of complete forgiveness we incarcerate ourselves in a prison cell of fear and doubt which is unbelief.

Several years ago I counseled a college student who had been sexually involved with her boyfriend. She had confessed her sin to God, sought forgiveness from her boyfriend, and even shared the pain of her failure with her parents. Yet for several years after her sin, she would repeatedly plead with God for His forgiveness. She suffered many personal, spiritual, and interpersonal consequences because of fear-induced doubt. It took several sessions of counseling before she realized that, even though she continued to feel regret and remorse over her sin, God had forgiven her and actually "remembered them no more" (Jeremiah 31:34); in fact, "As far as the east is from the west, so far has he removed our transgressions from us" (Psalm 103:12). That's a long way.

Finally, this young lady experienced freedom from doubting God's grace and forgiveness. She was able to accept the fullness of God's forgiveness and was set free from the doubt-initiated bondage of fear.

It is not humanly possible to forget many things in our past. Our minds were created by God in such a way that everything is permanently stored. But the good news is that God has granted us tremendous freedom to decide what to do with the memory. While the Enemy will use our memories to wear us out with fear, guilt, and doubt, God will use them as timely reminders of His absolute faithfulness, limitless forgiveness, and ultimate truth.

The choice is not whether or not you remember your sin; rather, it is whether you choose to let the memory of your sin help you to grow and change, or let it cause you to doubt God and yourself. Don't keep reminding God of your sins; He doesn't remember them any more. Let your memories of past failures trigger a spirit of praise and thanksgiving for God's gracious forgiveness and thorough restoration— there is just no doubt about it!

FREE AT LAST

I'm free from the guilt that I carried,
From the dull empty life I'm set free;
For when I met Jesus, He made me complete;

He forgot the foolish man I used to be.
I'm free from the fear of tomorrow;
I'm free from the guilt of the past;
For I've traded my shackles for a glorious song;
I'm free, praise the Lord, free at last![1]

Fear Creates The Illusion Of Perfection

Perfectionism—not the good kind that the New Testament says we all must strive for, but the kind that drives people to try to maintain complete control—is the fourth symptom of fear-induced distorted thinking. Because we are afraid, we try to control our own circumstances as well as those of people who are close to us. Our distorted thinking assumes that we can avoid fear if we keep everything under control. Perfectionists seem to expend excessive amounts of energy trying to maintain control. Gymnast Christy Henrich was a perfectionist, and in her fear of failure, she looked for complete control of her situation. This need for control involved her eating and her obsession with her weight. Christy's fiance, Moreno, said "I can remember Christy telling me 'there's only first place.'" In 1994 this striving for perfection and the resulting anorexia cost Christy her life.[2] Unfortunately, it is not humanly possible to regulate every circumstance of our own lives, let alone the lives of others.

Ironically, trying to live a perfect life often leads to a fear-dominated life. Fear and control seem to feed on each other—fear creates the need to control, but the struggle for complete control generates intensive feelings of fear and frustration. This pattern of behavior is similar to an "obsessive-compulsive disorder." An obsessional thought, derived from fear, leads to some kind of compulsive behavior intended to exorcise fear. Compulsive behaviors usually center around a person's living or working space. One familiar example is compulsive hand washing like that of

Shakespeare's guilt-ridden Lady Macbeth.

It is truly difficult to imagine the enormous amount of energy required to insist on excessive orderliness and control in a disordered, ever-changing world. The thought distortion behind such behavior seems obvious—"I'm afraid that if I don't keep everything under control, and my life perfectly organized, I will not be worthy or adequate." Regardless of the terms we use to describe it—burnout, emotional breakdown, or psychotic break—when a person hits the wall, exhausted and emotionally broken, when control is no longer possible, it is a terrifying experience.

It was a small thing that tipped the scale for one woman in counseling. Everything in her life had to be in perfect order, under control. She could not even relax and go to sleep at night until all of her shoes, dresses, and blouses were in a specific order in the closet. One day she received a phone call from the soccer coach explaining that, because she had missed the application deadline by two weeks, her children would not be included in the sports program that season. She would be placed on the waiting list. Her boys lived for sports. She said good-bye, sat down, began to cry, then went into hysterics and had to be hospitalized overnight. There was no room in her emotional reservoir for this "out-of-control" disappointment. All of her life she had battled fear through her shield of control, and when her self-designed compromise was breached, fear literally overwhelmed her.

Fear Compels Us To Expect The Worst

Negatively anticipating a future experience is potentially more damaging than experiencing the perceived problem. Negative anticipation is attaching meaning to circumstances or future plans on the basis of past fearful experiences.

When Cindy, a college student, lost her father to

cancer, she began to experience an uncontrollable fear of premature death. She got into a habit of constantly monitoring her body symptoms and making excessive trips to doctors' offices, convinced that some disease was quietly preparing to snuff out her life. This fear strategy of the Evil One is countered by the writer of Hebrews. He says that Jesus died so that "he might destroy him who holds the power of death—that is, the devil—and free those who all their lives were held in slavery by their fear of death" (Hebrews 2:14-15).

We will all die some time. But to fear death every day of our lives causes us to lose out on the joys available to us while we are here on earth.

I can personally relate to the temptation of fear-saturated negative anticipation. My brother Larry, who is only one year older than me, had a mild heart attack two years ago. He had to be in the hospital for angioplasty, was given a special diet, and is now on medication. My father had a major heart problem last year. He too had to be hospitalized to have his arteries cleaned out. All three of my mother's brothers died of heart-related diseases. With that kind of family history it would be easy for me to become morbidly preoccupied with every heartbeat. After all, heart disease is on both sides of my family, I am a Type-A personality, and I love chips and salsa. I could actually experience more physical and emotional damage from fear-drenched negative anticipation than I might ever experience with actual heart problems. When painful and fearful things happen to us personally, or to someone close to us, it may take time to overcome the fear that it or something worse will happen again.

Since one of Satan's primary targets is our thinking and imagination, is it any wonder that the Bible contains more than 300 references to the mind? Paul assures us that, as Christians, we have the mind of Christ (1 Corinthians 2:16). Also, he says, "Do not conform any longer to the pattern of this world, but be transformed by the renewing of your mind. Then you will be able to test and approve what God's will is— his good, pleasing and perfect will" (Romans 12:2). In addition, he urges us: "Whatever is true, whatever is noble, whatever is right, whatever is pure, whatever is lovely, whatever is admirable—if anything is excellent or praiseworthy—think about such things" (Philippians 4:8). In this way "we demolish arguments and every pretension that sets itself up against the knowledge of God, and we take captive every thought to make it obedient to Christ" (2 Corinthians 10:5).

Peter likewise tells us to "prepare your minds for action; be self-controlled; set your hope fully on the grace to be given you when Jesus Christ is revealed" (1 Peter 1:13). And Isaiah promised that God "will keep in perfect peace him whose mind is steadfast, because he trusts" in Him (26:3).

We are expected to manage our thoughts and to begin to relinquish the compromises of distorted thinking. Our mind needs to become saturated with Scripture, thereby conforming to the mind of Christ. Paul tells us that we can find shelter from anxiety's barrage by praying about "everything": "Do not be anxious about anything, but in everything, by prayer and petition, with thanksgiving, present your requests to God. And the peace of God, which transcends all understanding, will guard your hearts and your minds in Christ Jesus" (Philippians 4:6-7). There it is! God's peace, in Jesus Christ, will guard your mind from compromising. Like a fortress shields those within, prayer will protect you from the flaming arrows of fear-saturated thoughts which the Evil One shoots at you.

A chorus I can remember from the days of my youth ministry captures the goal in doing spiritual battle in the mind and imagination. It goes like this: "Lord Jesus, think Your thoughts through my mind, speak Your words through my lips, live Your life through my body, every hour of every day, till I see You face to face." Committing ourselves to think God's thoughts, to renew our minds in Christ Jesus, to bring every fearful thought into captivity, to flood our minds with God's wonderful Word will adequately equip us to harness fear-saturated thought patterns. What an incredible blessing and privilege to take on the characteristics of Christ in my mind, thoughts and imagination. And after a lifetime of growth and maturity, I can have the mind of Christ.

PERSONAL EVALUATION

1. I see now that the Enemy has distorted my thinking in the following ways: (circle the ones that bother you)
   - (a) thinking irrationally (bouncing between behavior/feelings/thoughts)
   - (b) rationalizing (compromising for safety's sake)
   - (c) doubting God's power in my life
   - (d) striving for perfection
   - (e) avoiding things or situations I cannot control
   - (f) expecting the worst (my worst struggle is with _____)

2. The one(s) that give me the hardest time is/are
_____ (describe in detail).

PRACTICAL APPLICATION

1. Select one of the distorted thinking patterns you listed above and compare it to God's truth, not your fears. For example: If I did not _____, (fill in from the list above), I would _____.

2. Memorize Philippians 4:6-7: "Do not be anxious about anything, but in everything, by prayer and petition, with thanksgiving, present your requests to God. And the peace of God which transcends all understanding, will guard your hearts and minds in Christ Jesus." Replace "anything" with your particular problem and pray the verse every day.

3. Tell yourself: Beginning today, each time I find myself falling back into one of the distorted thinking patterns listed above, I will stop and pray that God will help me break this pattern by His strength, not mine. Then, as Paul says, I thank God in Christ Jesus for delivering me from this fear.

PRAYERFUL MEDITATION

1. FEAR NOT—God promises to be with me when I am facing fear.

> *"Do not let this Book of the Law depart from your mouth; meditate on it day and night, so that you may be careful to do everything written in it. Then you will be prosperous and successful."*
> —Joshua 1:8

2. FEAR NOT—God promises peace as I concentrate on Him.

> *"You will keep him in perfect peace, whose mind is stayed on You, because he trusts in You."*
> —Isaiah 26:3

3. FEAR NOT—God promises to protect me.

> *"Do not be afraid. Stand still, and see the salvation of the LORD, which He will accomplish for you today . . . The LORD will fight for you, and you shall hold your peace."*
> —Exodus 14:13-14

Note:
[1] "I'm Free," by William and Gloria Gaither. © 1968 by William J. Gaither.
[2] Noden, Merrell. "Dying to Win." *Sports Illustrated*, August 1994. 55-64.

chapter

Fear Disrupts Our Emotions

The next major symptom of unharnessed fear is "disrupted emotions." There are more than 650,000 psychiatric admissions each day; emotional and mental illness parallels the problems of AIDS and cancer. Suicide is the third leading cause of death among teenagers. Anti-anxiety and anti-depression medication requires 230 million prescriptions each year. Stress-management seminars, tapes, and books are multi-million dollar industries. All of this is symptomatic of people trying to cope with crises, conflicts, anxiety, anger, worry, and other disruptive situations and emotions that contribute to a destructive lifestyle. And enmeshed with the whole gamut of these emotions is fear.

I met Jonathan when I was assigned a limited internship at Camarillo State Hospital while working on my doctoral program. Jonathan, like so many patients, displayed a wide variety of emotional symptoms that were directly related to fear.

Jonathan was an articulate and physically attractive man whose success in banking and investing had contributed to a beautiful home, a boat, a lake cottage, and many friends. His family was close knit and his marriage solid. When our nation's economy took a nose dive, Jonathan's financial strategy failed due to circumstances mostly outside of his direct control. He hit the wall emotionally. He was harassed by frequent anxiety attacks, excessive worry, outbursts of anger, and a prevailing depression that put his life in slow motion so that he wrestled with thoughts of suicide. His friends and family attributed it to mid-life crisis, burnout, or maybe just a temporary chemical imbalance. But all of these symptoms were in some way triggered by the tormenting fear of losing all that he had worked so hard to gain. The manipulating fear resulted in his emotional breakdown and eventual hospitalization.

As Jonathan related his story I could see the pain and almost feel the fear that still gripped him. The good news is that by this time Jonathan had recovered much of his emotional balance and would soon be discharged.

Not all stories about fear result in such dramatic consequences; however, whether mouse-size or mountain-size, each is in some way a tragedy of the human spirit. Unharnessed fear triggers and magnifies other major emotions. Not all emotions, of course, are triggered by fear, but generally, anger, anxiety, depression, and worry are often symptoms of an underlying fear. "I am anxious because I fear . . . " "I am angry because I fear . . . " "I am depressed because I fear . . . " "I am worried because I fear . . . " Perhaps even now in your own life you are experiencing emotional struggles and have never considered that fear could be a major contributor to that emotional problem. Like Jonathan, each of us has an emotional threshold limit, and when it is violated we experience major difficulties. Unharnessed fear, no matter how it manifests itself, can push us to the very limit of our emotional threshold.

In the field of engineering the threshold for handling stress is defined by the limits of a material's ability to carry loads or withstand force. The same is true of us. We each have limitations. In engineering, a metal's response to stress is determined by its chemical make-up. For example, some steels will bend easily. Others, like alloy steels, will withstand higher pressures without bending. A metal coat hanger bends easily without breaking. A razor blade (high alloy steel) won't bend at all but will fracture when stressed to its limit. It is the same with the human ability to handle fear-inducing stressors in life. Our responses are, to some extent, determined by our individual characteristics; obviously, some people can take more than others.

The Israelites' 40-year desert trek to their promised land was a mine field of fear booby traps. They started their journey being afraid of the Egyptians behind them and ended it by fearing the giants ahead of them. Both the people and their leaders stumbled over, tripped through, and got bogged down in anxiety, anger, worry, and depression, much of which could be traced back to fear. Just a casual review of these dramatic stories and prominent emotions easily spotlights four primary fear-related emotions.

Fear Interacts With Worry and Anxiety

The Israelites were chronically worried about how their needs would be met and how they would get to their destination. Just a few days after their miraculous escape across the Red Sea, after Moses' and Miriam's wonderful songs of praise to God, the people showed their worry and anxiety. "Then Moses led Israel from the Red Sea and they went into the Desert of Shur. For three days they traveled in the desert without finding

water. When they came to Marah, they could not drink
its water because it was bitter. So the people grumbled
against Moses, saying, 'What are we to drink?'" (Exodus
15:22-24). That began a long and relentless habit of
complaining and grumbling, reflecting fears couched
in anxiety and worry. They complained because they
did not have the same food they ate in Egypt, or
enough water, and were in constant danger from the
inhabitants of the lands they had to pass through.

Anxiety seems to be the official emotion of our
age, the basis of all neuroses, and the most pervasive
psychological phenomenon of our time. It is as old as
human existence, but the complexities and pace of
modern life have alerted us to its presence and probably increased its influence.

Fear-motivated worry is illustrated by putting a car in
neutral and racing the engine. Constructive concern is
putting the car in gear and moving toward your goal.
Carol Kent, in her book *Taming Your Fears*, depicts the
power worry can have in our lives when she says,
"Worry and anxiety give a small thing a big shadow."[1]

No wonder Jesus often taught about the importance
of not allowing fear to take control of our lives.
Unharnessed fear feeds worry and anxiety. Worry and
anxiety are frequently symptoms of fear that we have
permitted to maintain a stronghold in our hearts and
minds. How kind of God to put in His wonderful Word:
"Do not be anxious about anything, but in everything,
by prayer and petition, with thanksgiving, present
your requests to God. And the peace of God, which
transcends all understanding, will guard your hearts
and your minds in Christ Jesus" (Philippians 4:6-7).

Fear Inflames Anger

Not all anger is fear-related or fear-motivated. But
when we have a chronic short fuse and are prone to
an angry spirit, often it is a result of a specific fear in

our lives that we have not dealt with. It does not take long for fear to grow into full-blown emotional outbursts. Although not likely fear-related, a man in Bellevue, Washington provides an excellent illustration of an angry outburst. During a winter storm, he was driven to "autocide". That's what Major Jack Kellem of the Bellevue police department called the strange case of an irate motorist who beat, then shot his car after it got stuck in six inches of snow. Police said the man became so angry when his vehicle got stuck that he pulled a tire iron from the trunk and smashed all the windows. Then he hauled out a pistol and shot all four tires, reloaded, and emptied half of a second clip of bullets into the car. "He killed it," Kellem said. "It's a case of autocide." Kellem said the man was sober and rational but very angry.[2]

Fears can generate anger, and anger out of control clearly generates increased fears. Destructive anger, triggered by fear, haunts all of us. Every day, newspapers and TV relate incidences of anger erupting into disastrous results. A man attacks his neighbor because he fears that the neighbor's new driveway infringes on his property. A woman slashes all the tires on her husband's car, parked in the "other woman's" driveway, because she fears losing her husband. A political candidate maligns the character of his opponent because he fears the loss of power. The fear-filled personality adopts a corrupted golden rule: "Do to others before they can do to you." The people in these news stories were all manipulated by fear which triggered angry responses.

I recall an occasion when a client of mine lived out this fear-anger-fear cycle. If possible, I routinely take a Sunday afternoon nap. One Sunday afternoon I was just getting into a comfortable nap when the phone rang. On the other end of the line a very angry man was screaming at me. Momentarily stunned, I soon realized it was one of my counselees. He and his wife were having a fight and he demanded that I meet them at the office or he would hurt her "big time." As I drove into the office parking lot I saw the husband standing at the passenger side of their car, berating his wife. I assumed that when I drove up, things would take on a delightfully calm and clinical atmosphere. I was wrong. In the office he continued to verbally abuse his wife despite my persistent objections. Finally I cried, "That's enough!" Then I added, "Let me show you how that feels." I placed a chair right in front of him, stood on it, put my finger in his face and began to bellow, "How arrogant and unkind of you to verbally abuse your wife and totally disrupt this session. Now shut your mouth until I tell you to talk. I will be the one who decides how this session will be conducted!"

I rather enjoyed that moment of power, and you can imagine the reaction of the shocked couple. Although I did not hear an "amen" from his wife, her nonverbal cues indicated that she did not want me to stop. As I stepped down from the chair, I noticed that the man's chin was quivering. Being a veteran coun-selor, I knew that the quivering chin syndrome could be interpreted in one of two ways. Either my little demonstration had wonderfully connected with his heart and he was about to experience, for the first time in his life, a new insight into the destructive nature of anger or he was so ticked off that he was going to explode all over the counselor. Fortunately for me, the first option prevailed. He suddenly realized how his wife must feel when he verbally attacked her. He was quite responsive and compliant for the balance of the session, for which I was deeply grateful.

This strong, emotionally explosive person was in many ways a little boy in a man's body. The thing that had triggered this angry outburst was fear. He feared losing his job, losing his marriage, and losing control of an otherwise well-ordered life. He was unable to be vulnerable and transparent with his wife, daughter, and employer. He confessed that his greatest fear was of losing his power. The only way he could think to react to the fear gripping his heart was to become angry at the one closest to him, his wife. There seemed to be a direct relationship between the intensity of his verbal abuse and his inner fears. He explained to me that "when I am pitching an angry fit, I no longer am aware of my feelings of fear and insecurity. I feel power and control."

Fear Invites Depression

Tim LaHaye, in his book *How to Win Over Depression*, states: "Between 50,000 and 70,000 people commit suicide each year, and we know that only a small percent of those who attempt suicide actually succeed. Investigation has revealed that more than half of these people were suffering from depression. The National Institute of Mental Health indicates that 125,000 Americans are hospitalized annually with depression, and another 200,000 or more are treated by psychiatrists. Dr. Nathan Kline of New York's Rockland State Hospital reports that many unrecognized cases of depression go untreated. Estimates reach as high as four to eight million annually."[3]

Chronic depression may be symptomatic of a prevailing fear that needs to be identified and resolved before emotional balance can be restored. It is no wonder that, in a generation that feeds on a frenzy of fear-inducing images, depression is one of the most prominent emotional problems in the nation. Dr. Gary Collins says, "Depression has been recognized as a common problem for more than 3,000 years. It is a worldwide phenomenon that affects individuals of all ages (including infants), appears to be increasing among teenagers and young adults, and disrupts the

lives of an estimated 30-40 million people in the
United States alone.

"Depression is known as the 'common cold' of
mental disorders and has been called 'the most wide-
spread, serious, and costly psychiatric disease afflicting
humankind today.'"[4]

In a more recent study of depression the MIT Sloan
School of Management Analysis Group, Inc. concludes
that "problems related to depression cost American
employers an estimated $43 billion annually. Related
absenteeism from the work place alone contributed
more than $12 billion in losses. Other factors that
added to loss were lowered productivity, safety risks,
accidents, suicide and the cost of inadequate or inappropriate treatment."[5]

Living with fear for a long period of time creates an
atmosphere in which depression can thrive. Many of
the psalms show how fear and depression are related.
David expressed this fear-depression relationship in
Psalm 55: "O God, do not ignore my plea; hear me
and answer me. My thoughts trouble me and I am dis-
traught. . . . My heart is in anguish within me; the terrors of death assail me. Fear and trembling have beset
me; horror has overwhelmed me" (Psalm 55:1-2, 4-5).
This psalm from the pages of David's life came at a
time when fear and depression were his frequent
companions.

While traveling in Germany with a ministry team
from Christian Heritage College, I spoke at a military
chapel one Sunday morning. A lady came forward at
the invitation, obviously very anxious. She described
to me in great detail how this was the first time she
had attended church since her mother's sudden death
and funeral service in a local church. Since that time
her life had been an emotional roller coaster. For 18
months she had experienced anxiety attacks, anger,
excessive worry, and prevailing depression. She was

on medication but had made no attempt to get counseling. She came to the service because a friend in the community told her a psychologist was speaking.

All of the emotional symptoms she experienced were legitimate. She was able to gain a new sense of hope when she identified the core contributor to her disrupted emotions as fear—her fear of death.

It is helpful when experiencing disrupted emotions to ask yourself some important questions about any prevailing fear that has not been identified or dealt with. The more we understand the intimate relationship between fear and other emotions, the more we appreciate the emphasis in the Bible on trust, faith, hope, and love as antidotes to fear. These Biblical principles and godly characteristics will be discussed in a later chapter.

God's Word thoroughly addresses the battle we all have with fear-generated negative emotions. He graciously and lovingly motivates us to understand and apply His clear instructions to put off anger, bitterness, wrath, malice, hatred, worry, fear, anxiety, guilt, and covetousness. These will surely hurt you and those around you.

Spiritual traits that are health producing and contagious are God's powerful antidotes to negative, sinful emotions. Imagine the freedom and strength that result when we commit ourselves to developing spiritual fruit and other positive emotional and spiritual characteristics. Put on love, joy, peace, longsuffering, kindness, goodness, faithfulness, gentleness, self-control, gratitude, thanksgiving, and a spirit of encouragement. Fill your heart with these powerful spiritual ingredients and you will find there is little room for fear-generated negative emotions. Little by little, over your lifetime journey with God, commit yourself to gradually, carefully, and faithfully cultivate Christ-like control of your emotions.

PERSONAL EVALUATION

1. Looking back on yesterday I probably spent _____ minutes/hours and a lot of energy on worry and anxiety. This is pretty much the daily pattern of my life.

2. I do/do not have a "short fuse."

3. I know that I get depressed and discouraged:
   (a) frequently
   (b) somewhat
   (c) hardly ever

Take 15 minutes to work on the practical application questions on the next page.

PRACTICAL APPLICATION

1. Make a "worry" list and share it with your spouse or a close friend. Ask him/her to pray specifically every day for a week about one item on the list. At the end of the week share with your confidant about your success at turning this worry over to the Lord. Next week choose another item and do the same thing. Memorize Matthew 6:25 "Therefore I tell you, do not worry about your life, about what you will eat or drink; or about your body, what you will wear. Is not life more important than food, and the body more important than clothes?"

2. Think of the last time you lost your temper or became excessively angry at something or someone. Now see if you can trace that anger back to some specific, contributing fear.

3. Try to draw a direct line between your depression and a possible fear-generating source.

PRAYERFUL MEDITATION

1. FEAR NOT—God promises to provide your needs.

*"Therefore I tell you, do not worry about your life,
what you will eat or drink; or about your body,
what you will wear. Is not life more important than
food, and the body more important than clothes?"*
                                         —Matthew 6:25

2. FEAR NOT—God is always present with you.

*"Have I not commanded you? Be strong and
courageous. Do not be terrified; do not be discouraged, for the LORD your God will be with you wher-
ever you go."*
                                         —Joshua 1:9

3. FEAR NOT—Face your fears daily; the Lord will be
with you.

*"You will not have to fight this battle. Take up
your positions; stand firm and see the deliverance
the LORD will give you . . . Do not be afraid; do not
be discouraged. Go out to face them tomorrow,
and the LORD will be with you."*
                                         —2 Chronicles 20:17

Notes:
[1] Kent, Carol. *Tame Your Fears and Transform them into Faith, Confidence and Action.* Colorado Springs: NavPress Group, 1993: 55.
[2] *International Herald Tribune,* 19 January 1982.
[3] LaHaye, Tim. *How to Win Over Depression.* Grand Rapids: Zondervan Corporation, 1974: 16.
[4] Collins, Gary. *Christian Counseling, A Comprehensive Guide.* Dallas: Word Publishing, 1988: 78.
[5] "Depression is a Treatable Illness." *Personally Speaking.* September 1995:1.

chapter

Fear Has the Power to Damage Our Bodies

In the previous chapters we noted how fear can distort our thinking and disrupt our emotions. In this chapter we will see how unharnessed fear can actually cause negative changes in our physical health and damage our bodies.

In a class on abnormal psychology that I teach at Christian Heritage College, one of the most intriguing sections in our curriculum has to do with the relationship between our minds, emotions, and bodies. Students are asked to digest such terms as psychosomatic, somatoform, psychogenic, and psychophysiological. Each of these tongue twisters relate, in some fashion, to our body's response to our emotions. They indicate that the real pain we feel in some part of our body may not be triggered by a physical illness or abnormality but, rather, by an unharnessed emotion. And often this unharnessed emotion is fear.

John and Mary seemed to be a relatively stable couple. John was a very successful salesman, Mary was involved in the church, and their children were in college. One cold, wintry morning, while Mary was cleaning out John's suitcase after his return from a business trip, she discovered receipts for a gift and a motel reservation for two. Her immediate and perhaps reasonable assumption was that her husband might have been with another woman on the trip. She was traumatized by the thought. When Mary was a teenager her father had been unfaithful to her mother, resulting in divorce; since then, she had a prevailing fear that someday the same thing could happen to her marriage. Her preoccupation with the past, coupled with her so-far unfounded suspicions, took over and in time she became very ill. Eventually, a form of paralysis set in and Mary temporarily lost the ability to walk. And to make matters worse, she became very depressed.

After consultation with a host of specialists, it became apparent that Mary's difficulty was psychophysiological. Her emotional pain was converted to a physical paralysis. The road to recovery was related to understanding the meaning of the message sent to her through her physical symptoms. In time, with extensive counseling, she regained the full use of her legs. More importantly, she and her husband began to work on their relationship. Although this example dramatizes exaggerated physical symptoms, it clearly indicates how the power of the mind and emotions can impact the body.

No doubt, most readers of this book will not be

able to identify with the serious nature of this story. However, without exception, we can all identify some physical difficulties that are emotionally fueled.

Psychosomatic debilities are not uncommon. Even Dr. Luke in the New Testament linked fear and ill health when he talked about people fainting from fear of the terrible events of the tribulation (see Luke 21:26). Modern researchers agree that there is a direct connection between the brain, the nervous system, and the rest of the body. Here's how it works.

When we are faced with a threat, fear triggers the production of adrenaline and other stress hormones that prepare the body to fight or flee the impending danger. This defensive reaction increases the blood sugar, heart rate, blood pressure, and muscle tension, all of which provide the extra energy required for emergency actions. But if the sensation of fear persists once the emergency has passed, this extra energy remains. Our heart rate, blood pressure, and muscle tension continue on an elevated plane, and that which was intended for "emergency use only" begins to cause harm to the body. Constant tension raises the risk of illness.

Perhaps you have visited doctors over a span of years for various physical pains, and then your physician kindly suggested that you consider counseling. The suggestion probably offended you or hurt your feelings. But it is very true that your emotions, especially fear, can make your body sick.

Fear and Your Heart

As in many medical facilities across our nation, patients at Duke University Medical Center are taught to manage disruptive emotions such as hostility, anger, and fear which dramatically impact their overall physical well-being, but especially affect their hearts.

I will never forget the time I was sitting in a crowded Atlanta airport. Because bad weather had delayed multiple flights, people packed the entire area, filling the chairs, sitting on the floor, and leaning against the walls. Even though the noise made it difficult to concentrate on the book I was reading I finally zoned everything out. Suddenly someone grabbed me from behind and yelled in my ear! Talk about a heart rush! I let out a blood-curdling cry and just barely avoided propelling my book into the lap of the lady across from me, who also jumped and shrieked. In fact, everybody in the immediate area was momentarily startled.

I leaped to my feet and prepared to defend myself. To my surprise and great delight, there stood my pastor and friend, Dr. David Jeremiah! My first thought of "where did he learn how to behave that way?" was replaced with the realization that I had been his faithful teacher for many years: I had been startling him regularly. He stood there in the waiting room laughing with great gusto. I wouldn't have thought that a man of the cloth could enjoy "payback time" so much!

As we said, a temporary burst of heart-racing is normal and natural, equipping us for fight or flight. After discovering that it was my friend who frightened me, I made a decision to continue my plans for flight and not fight. However, a heart that continually races will begin to weaken. Being on continual alert contributes not only to the possibility of an initial heart attack but increases the potential of a second one.

Dr. Thomas Delbanco, Director of the Division of General Medicine and Primary Care at Beth Israel Hospital in Boston and Associate Professor of Medicine at Harvard Medical School, was interviewed by Bill Moyers. During the discussion Delbanco affirmed that when cardiac arrest patients are informed about their disease, the dynamics of a heart attack, and the probabilities of further heart problems, they become less fearful and fewer suffer a second heart attack. Moyers inquired, "Are you saying that their fear affects their bodily well-being?" Delbanco answered, "I'm sure of that." Moyers then asked if medical experts have always been aware of that. Delbanco suggested that what we have known intuitively for a long time is finally now getting the serious consideration of researchers.[1]

Fear and Cancer

Maggie Scarf, in an article in *Psychology Today* in 1975, wrote about Dr. C. Simonton and his psychologist wife and their theory on cancer-prone personalities. "The Simontons argue there is a cancer-prone personality, that certain combinations of emotional traits make people especially vulnerable to cancer."[2]

Simonton listed these characteristics in the article: "First, a great tendency to hold resentment, and marked inability to forgive; (2) a tendency to self-pity; (3) a poor ability to develop and maintain meaningful long term relationships; and (4) a very poor self-image." Although the emotion of fear is not specifically mentioned in this research article, it does clearly illustrate how negative emotions can contribute to serious physical problems.

"These qualities," Simonton proposes, "make it difficult for a person to deal with emotions at a constant level, to acknowledge negative feelings and then to deal with them." The feelings which the Simontons term "Negative Emotions" are eventually given somatic expression. Malignancy is thus despair that has been experienced biologically, despair at the level of the cell.[3]

If the Drs. Simonton research has validity, then it does not take a great stretch of the imagination to realize the role that Christian faith can play in healing various kinds of emotionally rooted illnesses.

Faith leads to hope, which leads to love, which transforms personalities and grounds us in the security of God's love and acceptance.

Fear and Your Immune System

Psychoneuroimmunology, or PNI, is a relatively new branch of psychology and medicine that studies the correlation between the nervous system and the immune systems. It has been found that nerve endings work in cooperation with tissues that produce, develop, and store immune system cells. In addition, the immune system responds to chemical signals from the nervous system.[4]

Dr. Margaret Kemeny, Assistant Professor of Psychiatry and Biobehavioral Sciences at UCLA, did her postgraduate work on immunology and psychoneuroimmunology. Dr. Kemeny found that the normal, fearful response to sudden danger can have a positive effect on the immune system, creating an increase in the immune responses.[5]

Even though there is no definitive proof regarding the connection between emotions, immune function, and illness, studies over the last 30 years suggest that the way a person deals with chronic negative emotions can have a major effect on his risk of illness.

A study by Glaser and Glaser of the Ohio State University College of Medicine shows that people under stress—one of the results of fear—experience less activity of immune system cells, making them easier prey for lurking illnesses. In 1991, Sheldon Cohen of Carnegie Mellon University gave volunteers doses of a cold virus. Those who came down with colds had suffered the greatest degree of stress during the previous year. This investigation mirrors the classic study in the early 1960s involving the U.S. Navy, which revealed that the men who had faced the most seriously stressful situations during the previous year were more at risk of becoming ill during the present year.

When fear becomes a long-term response, the immune system begins to break down, causing people to become more vulnerable to disease.

Fear and Pain

Learning how to respond to the fear-generating circumstance of having a baby, and how to manage the physical response of pain, is one of the primary purposes of natural childbirth training. My wife and I took special classes in preparation for the birth of our second child to help manage the natural emotion of fear and thereby reduce the intensity of physical pain. Breathing, concentration, coaching, and physical preparation were all part of the process. However, our journey together during the birthing process was not quite as smooth as it should have been.

At one point Marlene began to hyperventilate. Her fingers were stiff, a tingling sensation persisted in her feet and hands, and she began to panic. But she did not have to face the panic alone. Her fearless and well-trained coach—that's me—was prepared for such an emergency. They had taught us that in the event of hyperventilation, we should place a paper bag over the mother's mouth and help her breathe into the bag. We had failed to notice, however, that the bag had a hole in it, and thus we were making the problem much worse. Even though I responded with precise confidence and followed my training procedures perfectly, Marlene's condition deteriorated. Now her whole body was stiff. Being highly trained in psychology, I detected that her confidence level in her coach had taken a nose dive. Once I accepted the reality that our plan was not productive, I did what any composed coach would have done: I yelled "NURSE!" at the top of my lungs. Despite this rather dramatic glitch, Marlene and baby daughter Kendra did quite well.

Now don't miss the point of the story. Natural childbirth classes significantly diminish the power of fear and result in reducing the experience of pain. Marlene's ability to manage her response to a very frightening and painful situation made a difference.

Fear and Recovery From Illness

Not only can emotions contribute to physical illnesses but the emotion of fear can significantly limit recovery from major physical problems. According to Dr. Thomas Delbanco, "Uncertainty is the worst illness. The fear of the unknown can really be disabling. Even if the news is bad, people feel better if the uncertainty is dispelled." Based on this observation, he takes time to educate his patients about their illnesses and treatments. Fewer fears mean faster healing.[6]

My parents live on a farm in Ohio. On a cold winter night, a fierce arctic storm had covered the roads with ice, making traveling nearly impossible. Dad began to have pains in his arm and chest and was having trouble breathing. Mom called 911. But with the severe weather conditions, it took nearly two hours for the emergency team to get Dad to a hospital. He was in stable condition. They transferred him to a hospital in Columbus where the doctors decided to do a new procedure using a rotoblater to clean out his arteries. He was awake and heard the doctor say that they had inadvertently cut an artery. The surgeon asked Dad's permission to do open-heart surgery if necessary. Talk about fear! The medical staff fortunately responded with precision and were able to stop the bleeding without opening Dad up. Now the challenge for Dad, and thousands like him, is to deal with post-event fears in a way that provides him with the best opportunity for full recovery. For some people, every physical symptom becomes an alarm that they are having another heart attack. Fear of future heart attacks actually contributes to the potential of a recurrence. Little by little Dad has learned to deal with his fear-saturated experience with a growing confidence and faith that is health-producing and works as preventative medicine.

Psychiatrists at the Stanford University School of Medicine noticed a link between the alleviation of long-term fear in women with breast cancer and their overall health and recovery. They compared two groups of women with advanced cases of breast cancer. The members of one group did not participate in any support group. The others joined a support group where they could share common fears and anxieties. The outcome was that those in the support group experienced less nausea from the treatments and were generally healthier and lived longer.

Dr. Norman Cousins noticed this same bridge between attitude and positive emotions, and the ability to fight cancer. He observed that the person who leaves the doctor's office in a state of fear and panic has a greater struggle ahead of him than the person whose fears have been calmed. Dr. Cousins affirms that positive determination helps the body to produce its own "chemotherapy" in the fight for better health, even the fight against cancer.[7]

We must be somewhat cautious in this area. I am not talking about New Age medicine or non-traditional medical practices. The intricate and intimate relationship between the mind and body is verified repeatedly; thus we may conclude that a caring environment and the calming of fears can affect body chemistry in a positive way.

Fear and Death

Most of us tend to agree with Woody Allen's statement that he wasn't afraid to die, he just didn't want to be there when it happened. Unfortunately, the advent of death is inescapable—no exceptions, though we may subconsciously cling to a contrary hope.

However, says the writer of Hebrews, "since the children [of God] have flesh and blood, he [Jesus] too shared in their humanity so that by his death he might destroy him who holds the power of death—that is, the devil—and free those who all their lives were held in slavery by their fear of death" (Hebrews 2:14-15).

Commenting on this passage in Hebrews, Leon Morris says:

> The defeat of the devil means the setting free of those he had held sway over, those who had been gripped by fear of death. Fear is an inhibiting and enslaving thing; and when people are gripped by the ultimate fear—the fear of death—they are in cruel bondage. In the first century this was very real. The philosophers urged people to be calm in the face of death, and some of them managed to do so. But to most people this brought no relief. Fear was widespread, as the hopeless tone of the inscriptions on tombs clearly indicates. Shakespeare sounded pretty hopeless when he had King Richard lament 'Of comfort no man speak! Let's talk of graves, of worms, and epitaphs' (776).[8] But one of the many wonderful things about the Christian gospel is that it delivers men and women from bondage to fear. They are saved with a sure hope of life eternal, a life whose best lies beyond the grave.[9]

Faith always eliminates fear, even fear of death. David expresses this faith in Psalm 23:4: "Even though I walk through the valley of the shadow of death, I will fear no evil, for you are with me." Solomon, in Proverbs 14:32, states that "even in death the righteous have a refuge." The Apostle Paul saw death as gain (Philippians 1:21).

I saw these truths demonstrated beautifully in the life of my mother when she, like Dad, faced a life-threatening situation. She loved the Lord and was living with what was diagnosed as a very rare (only three cases in medical history) type of cancer. I was in college when I received the shocking news. In the spring, with its promise of new life, it seemed that my mother was taking steps toward death. Yet, those from our church who visited her said that they would go into her room with a sense of fear and sadness but would return home with a light heart and increased faith. Mom knew all too well the prognosis, but she refused to allow the fear of death to rob her of the joy of her remaining time to live.

Mother went through surgery and made a remarkable recovery, described by her physicians as miraculous. Today she enjoys life with clear memories of her confrontation with a life-threatening disease.

When it is your turn to catch a glimpse of that pale horse, you may sense the arising of the specter of fear. But when its voice booms loudly in the recesses of your soul, clamoring for full and constant attention, the voice of faith (God's voice through His Word) will utter a firm "HUSH!" and fear will become mute. Then you can echo the Apostle Paul's song, "Death has been swallowed up in victory. Where, O death, is your victory? Where, O death, is your sting?" (1 Corinthians 15:54-55).

Laughter is Good Medicine

There is a proven relationship between our emotions, our bodies, and the positive impact of humor. In his article titled "Laugh Your Way to Good Health," Nick Gallo said, "New research shows that humor is good medicine and can actually help keep you in good health." He reports that William F. Fry, M.D., describes laughter as "inner jogging," and underscores its benefit to a person's cardiovascular system. People being manipulated by fear find that they seldom laugh.

Comparing laughter to exercise, Gallo points out that when a person laughs heartily, several physical benefits occur: a temporary lowering of blood pressure; a decreased rate of breathing; and a reduction in muscle tension. He reports that many people sense a "relaxed afterglow." Gallo concludes, "An enduring sense of humor, especially combined with other inner resources such as faith and optimism, appears to be a potent force for better health."[10]

Mr. Gallo's observation echoes a precept written thousands of years ago. King Solomon, to whom God imparted great wisdom, said, "A cheerful heart is good medicine, but a crushed spirit dries up the bones" (Proverbs 17:22). He also told us to replace our fear of circumstances with a reverential fear (awe) of the Lord, to quit leaning on our own understanding of the situation. "This," he said, "will bring health to your body and nourishment to your bones" (Proverbs 3:8). Solomon also wrote: "A heart at peace gives life to the body, but envy rots the bones" (Proverbs 14:30). Current research and our own observations concur with Solomon's wise observations.

I love to be around people who have a sense of humor and love to laugh. This true story, only slightly embellished by my imagination, is a good illustration of getting joy out of life with a sense of humor. Each year I teach at Moody Bible Institute in Chicago, and it has become a family expectation that I always pray for storms when I am in the Midwest. I am from Ohio and truly miss the excitement of a good storm. While on the way to Moody one year, I was visiting with my parents and sister and her husband in Circleville, Ohio. I had called ahead and reminded them that I would love a storm. Right after a wonderful dinner, I was on the front porch and began to see lightning in the west.

My Dad said there was no storm in the weather forecast and that it was likely just heat lightning. Not so. In just a few minutes, it began to rain, the wind was blowing, lightning flashing, and thunder rolling. It was absolutely great! We were joking about my prayers being answered when a huge flash of lightning hit a tree in the front yard, split off a limb and blew wood fragments all over the place. It was terrifying and wonderful at the same time! I later sent my sister a plaque to hang on the stump of the tree.

Kenny's Prayer Tower

Here remains the stump of a tree;
An indication of how God loves me,
I prayed for a storm to cheer my heart;
And the Lord sent a bolt of lightning
And blew this tree apart!

It is so important to be able to find ways to enjoy a laugh and see the humor of life. It is health-producing and contagious. As Arnold Glasgow reminds us, "Laughter is a tranquilizer with no side effects," or as Dr. Charles Swindoll suggests, "Maybe it's time to laugh again."[11]

More than other people, Christians should benefit from laughter because we have the greatest reason to be joyful. Our faith is firmly planted in God, and our optimism is based on the assurance that we are under His wise control. Don't be afraid to enjoy a hearty laugh—it's good medicine.

Thank God for His faithful instruction and encouragement regarding the relationship between our minds, emotions, and body. What great love. His admonitions to renew our minds and develop the fruit of the Spirit were meant not only for our spiritual maturity, but our overall personal joy and physical health. Praise God!

PERSONAL EVALUATION

1. Migraine headaches, backaches, sleeplessness can all be related to chronic fear. If your doctor has eliminated any physical disorder that could cause such problems, do you still suffer from any of these maladies on a recurring basis? Which one(s)? What fear could be a contributing cause (for example, worry over financial stress)? Write down the thing that may be causing your fear.

2. Think of the last time you were faced with fearful news or a frightening experience. How did you respond?
    (a) Did you deal with it and continue on with your life, or
    (b) Are you still trying to overcome its control?
How long ago did this incident happen? Is it time you rid yourself of the effects of this fear?

3. How often do you laugh? Is it possible that the absence of laughter could be slowing your ability to regain your health?

PRACTICAL APPLICATION

1. Not all physical problems are caused by emotional upheaval. However, the next time you have physical pain, take a few minutes to look back at the past couple of days to see if there are any possible emotional contributors. Write down those things that bother you that may be causing your body to react.

2. Biblical attitudes that are health-producing and contagious are love, joy, peace, patience, kindness, goodness, faithfulness, gentleness, and self-control (Galatians 5:22-23). Choose just one of these qualities and determine a specific way that you are going to begin developing it in your life today. Tomorrow, choose one more. At the end of each day try to recall how you displayed that particular spiritual trait. Before long you will have emptied the fruit basket and discovered a more fulfilling lifestyle.

3. Memorize Proverbs 3:7-8: "Do not be wise in your own eyes; fear the LORD and shun evil. This will bring health to your body and nourishment to your bones."

PRAYERFUL MEDITATION

1. FEAR NOT—God has promised to give us rest from the battles of life.

> *"For I am the LORD, your God, who takes hold of your right hand and says to you, Do not fear; I will help you."*
> —Isaiah 41:13

2. FEAR NOT—God will give you needed strength and a song in your heart.

> *"Surely, God is my salvation, I will trust and not be afraid; the [YAH], the LORD, is my strength and my song; he has become my salvation."*
> —Isaiah 12:2

3. FEAR NOT—God is with you even in the most serious times.

> *"Even though I walk through the valley of the shadow of death, I will fear no evil; for you are with me; your rod and your staff, they comfort me."*
> —Psalm 23:4

Notes:
[1] Delbanco, Thomas. "The Healing Roles of Doctor and Patient," *Bill Moyers, Healing and the Mind.* New York: Doubleday: 7-23.
[2] Scarf, Maggie. *Psychology Today,* September 1980: 37.
[3] Ibid. p. 37.
[4] Bovbjerg, Dana H. "Psychoneuroimmunology: Implications for Oncology?" *Cancer,* 1 February 1991: 828+.
[5] Kemeny, Margaret. "Emotions and the Immune System," *Bill Moyers, Healing and the Mind*: 195-211.
[6] Delbanco, Thomas. "The Healing Roles of Doctor and Patient," *Bill Moyers, Healing and the Mind*: 7-23.
[7] Cousins, Norman. "Tapping Human Potential." *Second Opinion,* July 1990. 56+.
[8] Shakespeare, William. *The Complete Works of Shakespeare.* Ed. David Bevington. Glenview, Illinois: Scott, Foresman and Company, 1980.
[9] Morris, Leon. "Fear of Death." *Expositors Bible Commentary: Hebrews - Revelation.* Vol. 12. Grand Rapids: Zondervan Publishing House, 1981: 29.
[10] Gallo, Nick. "Lighten Up: Laugh Your Way to Good Health." *Better Homes and Gardens.* August 1989: 31-2.
[11] Swindoll, Charles R. *Maybe It's Time To . . . Laugh Again.* Dallas: Word Publishing, 1992.

THE
SOURCES
OF FEAR

chapter

Inadequacies, Insecurities, and Infirmities

What in your life causes you to fear? Losing your job? Having your marriage deteriorate, or not getting married in the first place? Seeing your secret sins exposed? Having an accident? Getting AIDS or cancer? Dying? Trying to work through a personal problem without understanding what causes the problem is like trying to mop up water from an overflowing sink without turning off the faucet.

In the medical profession, most prescription medication is palliative, not curative—it stops the pain but generally does not deal with the source of the pain. For example, a person with an abscessed tooth can buy a prescription to stop the terrible pain, but in order to end the problem the doctor must repair or eliminate the offending tooth. Dealing with symptoms of personal problems or personal pain is critical and essential, but we must identify the underlying sources before we can achieve a long-term solution.

A book this size cannot provide a detailed index of all fear-causing situations, nor can it reveal the root causes of every fear we experience. But we can show that many of our fears can be traced back to three aspects of our fallen nature: inadequacies, insecurities and infirmities. Before we transition in our discussion to the solutions of our fears, we need to understand how most of our fears spring from one of these personal traits. Understanding the primary sources of fear helps us appreciate and apply God's solutions. As we begin to see ourselves as thoroughly adequate and completely secure in Christ Jesus, we will gradually gain spiritual stamina and strength that will help us overcome both our smallest and greatest fears. Now let's examine more closely these three primary sources of most of our fears.

Inadequacies Are A Primary Source of Fear

At times, religious broadcasts and financial success seminars give us the impression that we have no limitations, that all we have to do is hit the delete button on the word "inadequate" and we can leap tall buildings with a single bound. Inadequacy, in brief, is the predicament of having less than what is required—I get a flat tire on the freeway and lack a spare; or I invite a dozen guests for lunch and find only one can of soup in the cupboard. To be inadequate is to weigh our resources, abilities, and accomplishments against the requirements and to come up short. Nothing is so intimidating as to face a specific problem and become keenly aware of an absolute inadequacy to solve it.

This, of course, tends only to magnify the problem and extend the suffering.

In her book on fear, Carol Kent points out that fear of public speaking is routinely listed as the number one fear of people.[1] Most people just don't feel adequate. Depending on the year the survey is done, only fear of death occasionally unseats fear of public speaking. I can relate to feeling inadequate as a public speaker.

I can well remember finishing my doctoral program and assuming my ministry position in Fort Wayne. I was enthusiastic about counseling and spent hours each day helping people sort out the challenges they were facing. However, I was not at all comfortable as a public speaker. Although I had taught at the college level, it was much more intimidating for me to speak in a large church like Blackhawk Baptist in Fort Wayne, Indiana. Each year we had a summer Bible conference with some of the most capable communicators from around the country. My pastor asked me to speak four times the first summer I was on staff.

I will never forget my first time speaking. There were over 1,000 people at the service. I was so terrified. I began to sweat. My voice seemed to get higher as the message wore on. By the time I was ready to close in prayer I sounded like a soprano. Now, after speaking for many years and applying the principles of God's instruction on how to overcome personal inadequacies, I am able to speak without being hindered by self-conscious fears.

Moses is a good Biblical example of a person who felt inadequate because of this personal limitation, among others. When God was ready to send him to challenge Pharaoh and lead His people out of Egypt, He already knew that Moses would feel inadequate; after all, even though he spent the previous years of his life in Pharaoh's palace, for the past 40 years Moses had been tending sheep in the desert, not a good place to improve your public speaking and leadership skills. He had almost forgotten the Egyptian dialect; he no longer knew anyone in the palace, and he hadn't been very popular with his own people, the Jews, when he did live in Egypt. God knew that it would take something spectacular to get Moses' focus off his own inadequacies and onto His omnipotence. So on the "far side of the desert" God got Moses' attention by speaking to him from a bush that was on fire but was not being consumed (Exodus 3 and 4).

Even though the Eternal One performed more miraculous signs, revealing His own power and the divine resources which Moses would have at his disposal, Moses was still afraid. He reviewed his own resources, weighed them against what was expected of him, and decided that he was terribly inadequate. He said to God, "Who am I" to do such a thing? "What if they do not believe me?" "I am slow of speech and tongue." "Please send someone else" (Exodus 3:11; 4:1, 10, 13).

What are some of the things that magnify a sense of inadequacy in us and provoke fear? Two major concerns are (1) the expectations of others and (2) the expectations we have of ourselves.

The expectations of others magnify our inadequacies. We emulate Moses when we weigh our resources against the expectations of others. We never seem to have enough time, money, or energy to keep up with the demands of life. Important deadlines seem to fall on the day the youngest child comes down with chicken pox, and the married son calls to say his whole tribe is on the way for a week's visit. Added to that, the continual crises of the kids growing out of their shoes and the government wanting more taxes keep us exclaiming, "Lord, there's not enough of me to go around. I may not be slow of speech like Moses, but

I'm slow in everything else. Slow to keep up with the lawn, the house, the job, the kids—not to mention the church—friends. I don't even have time to relax, take a vacation, or pursue a hobby. It's beyond me, Lord. It's not that I *seem* inadequate; I *am* inadequate."

A father quietly rocks back and forth in his chair, stares with glazed eyes at the ceiling, and begins to calculate the cost of raising soon-to-arrive "Junior" from the birth certificate to the college diploma. And before he can say "$100,000 dollars," he starts to perspire, his pulse rate triples, and he begins to hyperventilate.

Putting our resources up against the requirements to achieve goals which others sometimes set for us provokes a dull, achy dread and fear. It is like seeing an emergency and not being able to do anything about it.

One afternoon in 1988, the quiet solitude of puttering in my garage was interrupted with a banging noise and shouts of alarm from across the street. I ran out to investigate and froze in my tracks. The neighbor's house was in flames! I could hear the loud sirens and blast-horns of fire trucks, but they weren't there yet. As a rush of adrenaline raced through my body, I ran into our house, grabbed the fire extinguisher and ran across the street. There I stood, first gazing at those angry flames engulfing the house, then looking down at the trifling cylinder in my hand. Frustrated, I turned around, walked back to my garage and just stood there motionless, as helpless as a fireman without a water hose, watching my neighbor's home burn to a shell. There was a real and immediate need. I was eager to help but lacked the resources. I thought I must feel like Moses did.

After a lot of persuasion and with God's help and the help of his brother Aaron, Moses eventually led the Jews out of Egypt. But that was not the end of Moses' challenges. Only a few days out of Egypt, after seeing the mighty Egyptian army and their horses

drown in the Red Sea, Moses faced his next dilemma.
Here he was, wandering around the desert, responsi-
ble for the well-being of 3 million thirsty people and
no water. Finally, they came across a brackish well at
Marah. As the people blasted Moses with grumbling,
God once again showed that even though Moses'
power was limited, God's was not. He showed Moses
a piece of wood to throw into the bitter well. When
Moses acted on God's command, an act which
required childlike faith, the water became sweet. An
entire nation witnessed the immutable reality that God
can go far beyond our own inadequacies and
resources in order to meet our needs. The source of
so much fear, our real and perceived inadequacies,
are an invitation to cultivate a greater faith, trust and
hope in God's ability to make up the difference.

Concern for personal needs magnifies our inadequacies. God is not limited by my meager bank account or
a bad month in retail sales. He does not depend on my
company paycheck or IRA (though He generally uses
such normal means to provide for my needs) any more
than He was limited by a desert without sufficient
drinking water. Paul assured the believers at Philippi,
"My God will meet all your needs according to his
glorious riches in Christ Jesus" (Philippians 4:19).

Remember the 5,000 men, and who knows how
many more women and children, who sat on a remote
hillside listening to Jesus? The disciples experienced
that heart-sinking fear when they realized that it was
getting late, the people were hungry, Jesus was not
going to send them away to find food, and they were
expected to take care of it. "That would take eight
months of a man's wages!" one of them commented.

Ignoring their protest, Jesus told them to tell the
people to sit down and prepare for a meal. When the
disciples realized that the only food available in that
huge crowd was one small boy's picnic lunch, five

loaves of bread and two fish, the great discrepancy between what they needed in order to obey Christ and what was immediately available caused them to feel even more inadequate. They recognized their own finite humanity and the impossibility that their pitiful resources would make any difference at all. But this compelled them to turn to the source of all things, Jesus, the Eternal, the Sovereign, Jehovah Jireh.

The name "Jehovah Jireh" (Yahweh yireh which means "the Lord will provide") was spoken by Abraham in Genesis 22:13-14. It is what he called the place where God provided a ram for sacrifice. Jehovah Jireh has not changed. His immutability assures us that He will provide our various needs today, just as He did for Abraham, Moses, and the disciples. When He makes a few fish and a little bread feed an army, we should let this truth capture our attention and quiet our insecurities and inadequacies. Personal inadequacies turn our hearts toward heaven.

I once had an opportunity to attend a "divinely-appointed workshop" on God's absolute adequacy when human resources are absolutely inadequate. It was quite frightening and wonderfully faith-generating. The college where I worked found it necessary to require faculty and staff to share in a temporary economic survival strategy. My employer had to cut salaries in half. With a full-time position at half-time pay, a California-sized house payment, a family of five to care for, and normal living expenses, I could now give a first-person testimony about the power of fear when faced with personal inadequacy. Like the disciples, my resources ran far short of the needs. And this happened while I was leading my first seminar on how to handle fear!

But the God of Abraham, Moses, and the disciples wonderfully and supernaturally provided for all our needs. One of our pastors learned of our financial pressure and gave a sacrificial gift to the Nichols family. My parents sent us enough money to cover our house payment, and other friends responded to our 911 call. Quite amazingly, at the end of that year when we were completing our income tax we discovered that our total annual income was equal to what it would have been before the salary cut. But of much greater value was the spiritual realization of how humanly fragile and inadequate we are and how wonderfully faithful and gracious our Heavenly Father is when we are faced with fear-drenched inadequacies. After the crisis months passed, my employer was able to reimburse us for the remaining salary.

Dr. Chuck and Lorretta Emert, two wonderful friends, are a great source of spiritual encouragement. Dr. Emert teaches in the Bible department at Christian Heritage College. Several years ago they too found themselves trying to stay afloat amid the choppy waters of financial adversity. They had some specific financial needs and did not have the resources. Chuck was walking along the beach very early one morning and noticed something near the water. When he reached into the water to pick it up, he discovered a billfold that had obviously been there for a long time. He looked through it, but found no identification. Later on after the billfold had dried he began to look through it more carefully and found a hidden compartment that he had not noticed before. It contained nine one-hundred-dollar bills! God had met their special needs when their own human resources had been depleted. Chuck was actually meditating and praying about their financial needs when the discovery was made. (Chuck and Lorretta seem to spend a lot of time at the beach now!)

Do you know why we feel so inadequate at times? Because we *are* inadequate. Routine issues and events will frequently exceed our human resources and our inadequacies can either become a primary source of fear or a timely reminder of God's wonderful power and presence. We see God most clearly when we look toward heaven with a heart being teased with fear.

Insecurities Are A Primary Source of Fear

Our feeling of inadequacy in handling present demands fits hand in-glove with our feeling of insecurity in facing the future, creating fertile soil for fears to grow.

Several situations in life can cause us to feel insecure and full of fear: (1) the "what-ifs"—negative anticipation of the unknown; (2) negative anticipation of the future, which to some extent is outside our control; and (3) what other people may think.

Often we suffer enormous emotional agony in worrying about events in life that we cannot influence or control. This unique source of fear is the malignant disease of the "what-ifs." We talked earlier about being "preoccupied, paranoid, and paralyzed" by fear. The paranoia dimension is directly tied to our insecurities about the unknown and unexpected events of life. Thoughts of an accident that might happen, a disease that lurks in the shadows, or a decision that could be a mistake all flow from our basic insecurities. And if we should forget for a while the potential dangers in our lives, the media will remind us. Vivid stories of violence, crime, murder, rape, drive-by shootings, and holdups make us painfully aware of our own vulnerability—which feeds our insecurities.

Most people spend much emotional and physical energy trying to deal with issues that are outside of their control and then are exhausted when it comes to important issues that are well within their control. Our legitimate concerns, which are a step or two removed from our direct influence or control, should be a prayer priority and we should take responsibility for the things that we can influence or control.

Recently, a young couple was sitting inside their car, parked on a main street beside a lighted tennis court, taking a break from the stress of college life, enjoying a cup of yogurt. Suddenly they found themselves in the middle of a drive-by shooting! The young lady was hit in the jaw and arm, the young man took a bullet in the mouth. Both were treated at a local hospital and have fully recovered, but can you imagine how many insecurities regarding personal safety can develop from such an experience?

FBI crime reports show that in America an automobile is stolen every 20 seconds, a burglary occurs every 10 seconds, a murder every 24 minutes. Statistics like these make us want to stay home with our doors locked and our windows barred. Even our own front yards can be arenas of danger. Emergency room statistics reveal that over 200,000 people a year are injured by lawn equipment. But inside the house isn't safe either. Kitchen equipment was the cause of over 800,000 accidents in 1988. Neither are we safe just sitting around the house and reading or watching TV because, in the last 10 years, 605 people lost their lives in tornados, 93 in hurricanes, and 1,244 failed to survive floods, not to mention those who died in earthquakes. Feeling insecure?

We face the same threat of crime, accidents, and natural disasters as the psalmist did, however, when he penned the words of Psalm 46: "God is our refuge and strength, an ever present help in trouble. Therefore we will not fear, though the earth give way and the mountains fall into the heart of the sea, though its waters roar and foam and the mountains quake with their surging. . . . The LORD Almighty is with us; the God of Jacob is our fortress" (v. 1-3,7).

The Lord quieted the psalmist's fears that stemmed largely from events outside his control, and God will do the same for us.

We cannot do anything in our own power to limit or prevent natural disasters (except protect ourselves by heeding storm warnings) and very little to curb evil deeds of the criminal element (maybe avoid dark alleys). But what about fear that comes from events that at least to some extent are under our control?

Uncertainties about the future generate insecurities. In my courtship and marriage class it is my privilege to help students become equipped for the dating and marriage process. Each year I counsel with those who have dated for an extended time and now face the question, "Is this person God's choice for a life partner?" They struggle with personal doubt: "Is this the man/woman I really love? Do I want to spend the rest of my life with him/her in marriage?" Insecurity about the future makes decision-making seem bigger than life. What if I make a mistake; marry the wrong person or miss marrying "Mister or Miss Right"?

It is easy to be propelled by the tail wind of fear and forget about the Source of all security. David reminds us that God is prepared to instruct us, teach us, and guide us (Psalm 32:8), directing us into paths of righteousness for His name's sake (Psalm 23:3).

Imagine the immense insecurities Gideon felt when he was faced with a divine appointment. The Midianites and the Amalekites had taken over his land, and the Israelites were afraid of theft and violence. Because times were so insecure, Gideon and his people hid in caves and stored their grain in underground bins. They were poor and oppressed, desperately in need of direction.

When the Israelites called upon God for relief, God sent a prophet to remind them of His past faithfulness. Then an angel visited Gideon (who was getting his wheat ready to hide underground at the time). The angel greeted Gideon with, "The LORD is with you,

mighty warrior" (Judges 6:12). These words spoken to
a farmer sound sarcastic to us, and Gideon must have
wondered why God was sending a divine messenger
to him. He asked, "But sir . . . if the LORD is with us,
why has all this happened to us? Where are all his
wonders that our fathers told us about . . . ? But now
the LORD has abandoned us, and put us into the hand
of Midian" (v. 13). A reasonable response in light of
the circumstances, wouldn't you say?

The angel wasn't there, however, to defend the
Lord's miracle business but to change Gideon's status
from insecure spectator to courageous participant. So
the angel said to Gideon, "Go in the strength you
have and save Israel out of Midian's hand. Am I not
sending you?" (Judges 6:14). Gideon was already fearful and insecure about the future because of the
Midianite's oppression and the decisions the nation
had to make. But now, as a path of action opened to
him, a new wave of fear washed over him. His
thoughts must have been, "Save Israel out of Midian's
hand? Who is this fellow? How do I know that God
sent him? Why would God expect me to do this
impossible thing?"

Gazing upon an uncertain future, Gideon's
response reflected his self-consciousness and insecurity as he answered, "How can I save Israel? My clan is
the weakest in Manasseh, and I am the least in my
family" (v. 15). He might as well have said, "I haven't
even so much as led a boy scout troop, let alone an
army. Surely when you said, 'mighty warrior,' you did-
n't mean me."

Perhaps by now Gideon was beset with another
fear—fear that God was going to be angry with him
because of his questions. He asked if he could bring
an offering to the Lord. The angel agreed and Gideon
killed and cooked a young goat, made broth, baked
bread and took it all out and set it under an oak tree.

Patiently the angel directed Gideon to put the meat
and bread on a rock and pour the broth over them.
When Gideon obeyed, the angel touched the meat
and "fire flared from the rock, consuming the offering"
(v. 19- 21). Gideon then knew that he stood in the
presence of the angel of the Lord. What others think
generates insecurities. This experience with an angel
of the Lord prepared Gideon for action. But when he
accepted his first assignment, he realized that his
adventure with fear would continue.

He was instructed to tear down the altar of the idol
Baal, build an altar to the God of Abraham, and offer a
sacrifice on it (Judges 6:26). This was a bold act, but
Gideon determined to obey the Lord. Then he realized
that even though he had partially conquered his fear
of Midian, he still had to deal with his family and the
townspeople. So he worked at night under the cover
of darkness. As morning light exposed the dastardly
deed, the men of the town called for an investigation.

When Gideon was identified and sentenced to
death, his father shamed the crowd into challenging
Baal to contend for himself. But Baal was having trouble with his hearing aid, so to speak. His response
was like that from a stone. Silence. Dead silence! This
incident boosted Gideon's courage and he began to
live with the assurance that the Lord was with him—
for a while anyhow, until lesson number two came
his way.

From the outset, Gideon was insecure and uncertain about his future, afraid every step of the way. But
his fear did not control him as it did the Midianites
when fear propelled them into total defeat. Because
the Lord was with Gideon, victory was guaranteed.
Proverbs reminds us, "The horse is made ready for the
day of battle, but victory rests with the LORD" (21:31).
Gideon was absolutely, positively, irrevocably, and
unalterably inadequate and insecure. But instead of

becoming consumed with his insecurities, he was confident in God's promises and presence.

Today we continue to feel the intense insecurity
brought on by the uncertainties of the future and our
inability to control them. We can either be overcome
by these fears or focus on the promises of God who
tears down our fears while building our faith. "Let the
beloved of the LORD rest secure in him, for he shields
him all day long, and the one the LORD loves rests
between his shoulders" (Deuteronomy 33:12).

Infirmities Are A Primary Source of Fear

In chapter four I developed the relationship
between unharnessed fears and its impact on our
physical health. In this section I want to place an
emphasis on how a focused fear of physical problems
is the third primary source of much emotional suffering. The dictionary helps us see more clearly exactly
what the word *infirmity* really means, especially as it
relates to fear. Infirmity refers to weakness in the
body and health, unsteadfast and faltering, not firm,
solid or strong. The meaning goes beyond the
boundaries of physical well-being. Those terms can
obviously create an atmosphere where fear can gain
a stronghold. Our inability or unwillingness to reconcile with our physical limitations and potential loss is
at the core of considerable fear-motivated suffering.

The urge to survive physically is God-given; we
naturally dread the thought of illness, incapacitation,
and death. Strangely, however, the very fear of physical limitations and chronic health problems, in turn,
causes physical problems ranging from migraine
headaches to seriously debilitating disorders. And fear
of death and illness is not limited to ourselves. We
fear for our loved ones as well.

But this is not the only kind of physical limitation
we are concerned with. We have also become victims

of society's obsession with a perfect physique, a flaw-less face and perpetual youth. Television provides a steady diet of persuasive propaganda which denies the reality of potential infirmities of any sort.

Is beauty really only skin deep? When it comes to appearance it seems we never quite measure up. Most of us probably have something about our bodies that we wish were different. And usually we become aware of the weakness when it is vividly pointed out in media ads that hawk the perfect body and face. But the social measuring device marketed through ads is in a constant state of change. What is "in" today may be "out" tomorrow. This feeling of not meeting soci-ety's idea of perfection is more than just skin deep; it can become a source of obsessive fear. The realization that no matter what the media markets as desirable, no matter how preoccupied we become with attaining and maintaining optimal health and a perfect physical appearance, we have unavoidable infirmities which create fear within us.

One way to quiet the underlying fears of aging, health problems or not measuring up to a culture that is saturated with a youth philosophy, is by surgically changing physical features. Cosmetic surgery, a multi-million dollar industry, is more popular than ever. Appearance-conscious teens and adults spend thou-sands and risk surgery to change any part of their bodies that can be changed. Noses, chins, and breasts are surgically redesigned and rebuilt. Body hair, cel-lulite, and wrinkles are removed. Heads of hair are bleached, hennaed, dyed, cut, or left to grow. What cannot be changed or removed is covered up.

In one year cosmetic companies spend 1.5 billion dollars on magazine and television advertising. Exercise equipment brings their manufacturers nearly two billion dollars. Spas, clubs and exercise programs are big busi-ness—all this to attain the perfect body and avoid not measuring up to the youthful and sexy ideals paraded before us by the media. Then, after investing mega bucks on trying to bring about physical perfection, we finally discover that the prevailing condition of our bodies is influenced by our genes and that life takes its toll on physical appearance and strength.

We can do a lot to improve what we already have, but perfection and the avoidance of various physical infirmities is beyond the reach of all of us. And if we are not discerning, it can be a major source of fear-related suffering.

Throughout Scripture God addresses our obsession with the external. In the famous Sermon on the Mount (Matthew 6:25-34), Jesus turns our attention from ourselves to the birds and the flowers. They have no eternal souls, they are worth little, they are here today and gone tomorrow—yet they possess unmistakable beauty and are well nurtured by their Maker. Then Jesus clarifies His application. "If that is how God clothes the grass of the field, which is here today and tomorrow is thrown into the fire, will he not much more clothe you, O you of little faith?" (Matthew 6:30).

When Samuel had wrongly assumed that Jesse's son Eliab should be the automatic choice as Israel's new king, God warned, "Do not consider his appearance or his height, for I have rejected him. The LORD does not look at the things a man looks at. Man looks at the outward appearance, but the LORD looks at the heart" (1 Samuel 16:7). Guess who was selected instead of Eliab? The younger shepherd lad, David. This son of Jesse had a heart for God.

Another feared infirmity is loss of physical freedom. Concern about our looks seems trivial when compared to a physical handicap. When freshman English students were asked what they valued most in life, eight out of ten answered, "Freedom to do as I wish and say what I want." But physical disabilities can hamper that freedom, and thus we dread them.

When a child's legs look funny and he can't walk as well as other children, he stands out like a neon light. The other children stare and mimic their little handicapped friend because of their own personal fears. Subconsciously they wonder, "What if this happened to me? How could I manage?"

Joni Eareckson Tada relates her fears as she became aware of the physical damage sustained by her body as the result of her diving accident. She experienced horror on the beach when she realized that she could neither feel nor move her limbs. In the hospital she felt horror as the hospital staff shaved her head. In surgery she felt panic that she might never see her family again. All of this dread came to a climax when the doctor informed her that she would never walk again. How could she manage? Her freedom, even to scratch her nose, was forfeited forever.

The Apostle Paul's freedom was likewise hindered by an infirmity. We don't know the nature of the problem, but he called it his "thorn in the flesh," and it caused him to plead with the Lord to take it away. Full use of his body was not restored, but he learned through his handicap, as Joni did through hers, that God's grace was sufficient; His strength could be perfectly displayed through weakness. Therefore Paul changed his attitude. Setting aside his fear of limitations, he accepted them as part of God's plan. "Therefore I will boast all the more gladly about my weaknesses, so that Christ's power may rest on me. That is why, for Christ's sake, I delight in weaknesses, in insults, in hardships, in persecutions, in difficulties. For when I am weak, then I am strong" (2 Corinthians 12:9-10).

Paul realized that being spiritually crippled was much more disabling than any physical defect. After pleading with God, he accepted the divine answer, even though he had hoped for a reversal. He allowed faith to displace fear, and he was able to proclaim with conviction, "Be joyful always, pray continually; give thanks in all circumstances, for this is God's will for you in Christ Jesus" (1 Thessalonians 5:16-18).

Infirmities? Sure, we all have them. But how are we handling them? Does focusing on our limitations quench the joy of life, or do we thank God for the capabilities we do have? Do we recognize that our weaknesses have strengthened us? Do we focus on His sufficiency or on our deficiency? The unsteady and faltering aspects of our physical make-up can be a great opportunity for spiritual growth.

Physical disability is not our only concern relative to these vulnerable bodies of ours. We monitor our health like a watchdog because disease and pain occasion other sources of fear. We check our cholesterol, eat vegetables, take vitamins, exercise, and get eight hours of sleep a night to preserve and perpetuate the good health we possess. In Japan people in the city streets and trains wear surgical-type masks to protect others and themselves from colds and flu. Not a bad idea, I guess, but a bit cumbersome.

Some fear ill health more than death itself. This kind of fear forms the very foundation for the philosophy of the Hemlock Society and other groups who propagate the rights to die, assisted suicide, and euthanasia. These ideas aren't new.

Wasn't this kind of fear expressed by Job's wife when she urged her very sick husband to "curse God and die!" (Job 2:9)? Job was sick because Satan himself had touched him. He was covered from head to toe with boils (2:7); the nights were long, uncomfortable, and sleepless (7:4); he endured wormy, dirty, open sores (7:5); he was in torment (30:17-19); and he burned with fever (30:30).

Job felt vulnerable. He had been living the good life, but then God seemed to turn on him, making

him a target for Satan's archers. He felt deserted—
even by God—depressed, and hopeless (16:12-16).

In a state of intense despondency Job exclaimed,
"What I feared has come upon me; what I dreaded
has happened to me" (3:25). He wondered why he
was born (3:11); he was even terrified of God (23:14-
16). His wife counseled, "Die with dignity, Job." But
then Job looked up through his fear with eyes of
faith and asked, "Shall we accept good from God, not
trouble?" (2:10).

David Ring was born with cerebral palsy. By the
time he was fourteen he had lost both of his parents.
Doctors said that David would probably never marry,
father children, or communicate effectively because of
his palsy. But today he has a lovely wife and four
wonderful children. David still has a damaged body
and halting speech, but he says that there is more
than one kind of miracle. He travels all over the country witnessing to his faith in Jesus, the great physician.
He sings:

I heard an old, old story, how a Savior came
    from glory,
How He gave His life on Calvary to save a
    wretch like me;
I heard about His groaning, of His precious
    blood's atoning,
Then I repented of my sins and won the victory.
I heard about His healing, of His cleansing power
    revealing,
How He made the lame to walk again and
    caused the blind to see;
And then I cried, "Dear Jesus, come and heal my
    broken spirit,"
And somehow Jesus came and brought to me the
    victory.
O victory in Jesus, my Savior, forever,

He sought me and bought me with His redeem-
ing blood;
He loved me ere I knew Him, and all my love is
due Him,
He plunged me to victory beneath the cleansing
flood. [2]

As David stands before thousands in his damaged
body, speaking with halting speech, there is no doubt
that he has true "victory in Jesus."

Thank God for His wonderful grace in providing
supernatural resources that equip us to overcome, little by little, our inadequacies, insecurities, and infirmities. We are truly being "perfected" in Christ.

PERSONAL EVALUATION

1. I know that I am self-conscious and insecure in some areas of my life. Three of the most prominent are:

2. I can identify at least one recent example of a situation or relationship that highlighted my feelings of inadequacy. That was when . . .

3. How do I typically respond to personal or physical infirmity? Is there an infirmity that I feel most? Have I grown spiritually by facing infirmities? Has someone close to me grown as a result?

PRACTICAL APPLICATION

1. Memorize Philippians 4:13: "I can do everything through him who gives me strength."

2. Write down three specific personal or family illustrations of being faced with a fear-drenched inadequacy, insecurity or infirmity and how God wonderfully met your needs far above all you could have asked or thought.
   a.   Problem

        Provision

   b.   Problem

        Provision

   c.   Problem

        Provision

3. Read one chapter of Exodus each day and identify themes of inadequacy, insecurity and God's response to His people.

PRAYERFUL MEDITATION

1. FEAR NOT—God will quiet my heart and meet my needs.

"Do not be anxious about anything, but in everything by prayer and petition, with thanksgiving, present your requests to God."
—Philippians 4:6

2. FEAR NOT—God will protect me from being dominated by anxiety when feeling insecure and inadequate.

"And the peace of God, which transcends all understanding, will guard your hearts and your minds in Christ Jesus."
—Philippians 4:7

3. FEAR NOT—God will faithfully take up the slack when our needs go beyond our abilities.

"And my God will meet all your needs according to his glorious riches in Christ Jesus."
—Philippians 4:19

Note:
[1]   Kent, Carol. *Tame Your Fears and Transform Them into Faith, Confidence, and Action.* Colorado Springs: NavPress Publishing Group, 1993: 55.
[2]   Bartlett, Eugene M. Sr. "Victory in Jesus," copyright 1939 by E.M. Bartlett. © Copyright 1967 by Mrs. E.M. Bartlett. Renewal. Assigned to Albert E. Brumley & Sons. All rights reserved. Used by permission.

SECTION
FOUR

THE
SOLUTIONS
TO FEAR

chapter

The Power of an Eternal Perspective

W hat can we do to harness the incredible power of fear? What is God's road map for our journey from living in fear to living by faith?

In the following chapters we will discuss the development of some primary spiritual and personal qualities that are at the core of lasting solutions to fear. We will chart a reasonable, attainable, Biblical plan that will direct you toward freedom from controlling fears and equip you to face the future with a new sense of confidence and courage. The plan dramatically illustrates the divine-human cooperative—you and God yoked together: God doing what requires supernatural power, and you committed to doing your part in a team effort that is guaranteed to lead to victory.

The first and foundational priority in working toward lasting solutions requires that you establish a fresh and vibrant perspective of God's limitless power and His divine plan to overcome fear. A consistent Biblical perspective opens the door for a thorough appreciation for God's faithfulness.

One day I was dressing for racquetball at a local club when a man who had just finished playing entered the locker room and proceeded to remove his prosthetic leg and put it in the locker. This surprised and inspired me, so I asked about his loss and evident recovery. A Vietnam war veteran, he had lost his leg in combat but testified to a comprehensive physical and emotional rehabilitation.

I wondered at the difference between this man and thousands of other veterans with identical backgrounds who still fill beds in VA hospitals or wander the streets of inner cities, homeless and hopeless. Obviously, it's not the loss of a leg or the availability of treatment programs. It must be the veteran's perspective that makes the difference, and perspective influences response. A person who is fear-manipulated gets up every day, looks in the mirror, and becomes obsessed with his disability. The one who responds constructively with the Biblical perspective recognizes, "Sure, I'm missing a leg but just look at what I have left." This is what Paul meant when he said, "Be joyful always; pray continually; give thanks in all circumstances, for this is God's will for you in Christ Jesus" (1 Thessalonians 5:16-18). Be thankful not *for* the circumstances but *in* them.

A proper perspective decreases fear and increases motivation. It does not restore the leg but allows one to face with courage and determination the fear of being handicapped. Let's identify and discuss Biblical principles that are prerequisites to cultivating a Biblical perspective.

Fear of God Cultivates A Heavenly Perspective

Perhaps part of developing a Biblical perspective requires us to recognize still another kind of fear, a positive fear even more powerful than motivating fear. We call it "consecrated fear." Consecrated fear has to do with loyalty, love, respect, reverence and obedience to our all-loving Almighty God, and is a "forever" fear. The call to fear the Lord recurs in Scripture more than 100 times.

Solomon tells us that the "fear of the LORD is the beginning of knowledge" (Proverbs 1:7). The psalmist adds that it is "the beginning of wisdom; all who follow his precepts have good understanding. To him belongs eternal praise" (Psalm 111:10). We also read that "to fear the LORD is to hate evil" (Proverbs 8:13); and the fear of the Lord "adds length to life" (Proverbs 10:27), and "is a fountain of life, turning a man from the snares of death" (Proverbs 14:27).

In some ways fear is able to manipulate us because we have neglected this consecrated fear of God. Perhaps, without a proper perspective of the Sovereign God, which indicates that we do not really take Him or His Word seriously, we tend to justify and rationalize our attitudes and behaviors. Getting set free from the bonds of controlling fear requires that we cultivate a new awareness and appreciation for Almighty God's power and presence. A reverential fear of God motivates us to faithful service, an obedient lifestyle, and an ever-growing disgust for sin.

Once we resolve to know God intimately and cultivate a reverential fear of Him as Sovereign, Almighty, Holy, and Everlasting, we get a proper perspective of fear, and we filter our fearful circumstances through our knowledge of God. This perspective may not diminish the reality of the problems, but it will give us courage and confidence to face them. This method of viewing life prompted me to establish the acronym for ALIVE Counseling Ministries—Always Living In View of Eternity (I Cor. 4:17-18).

Christian, you will be less vulnerable to the intimidating nature of fear if you cultivate an ever-increasing reverence and respect for our righteous and holy God. Fearing God, according to the Scripture, frees us from fearing what man (or anything else in this world) can do to us. How liberating! Remember Jesus' promise, "So if the Son sets you free, you will be free indeed!" (John 8:36).

God's Power Cultivates A Heavenly Perspective

Moses experienced God's power and the inseparable relationship between consecrated fear and obedience when he received the Law from God on Sinai. On the day the Lord God Almighty called Moses to the mountain,

> there was thunder and lightning, with a thick cloud over the mountain, and a very loud trumpet blast. Everyone in the camp trembled. Then Moses led the people out of the camp to meet with God, and they stood at the foot of the mountain. Mount Sinai was covered with smoke, because the LORD descended on it in fire. The smoke billowed up from it like smoke from a furnace, the whole mountain trembled violently, and the sound of the trumpet grew louder and louder. Then Moses spoke and the voice of God answered him (Exodus 19:16-19).

What an awesome experience. No wonder the Israelites stood at the base of the mountain in fear.

Exodus 20:18-20 reiterates that "when the people saw the thunder and lightning and heard the trumpet and saw the mountain in smoke, they trembled with fear. They stayed at a distance and said to Moses, 'Speak to us yourself and we will listen. But do not have God speak to us or we will die.'" However, Moses said to the people, "Do not be afraid. God has come to test you, so that the fear of God will be with you to keep you from sinning."

Seeing God's might, power, and greatness built a sense of reverence and awe into their lives and caused them to immediately renew their allegiance to Him. But it didn't last very long. Reverence and fear of God need to be nurtured and renewed daily. When the Israelites were able to get beyond God's reach, their awesome respect for His power began to fade. When that happened the people implored their priest, Aaron, to make a golden idol that they could see and handle and worship. Almighty God was up there on that terrifying mountain, not down in the wilderness. They wanted a god that they could manipulate, one that had no power to scare them to death. So, out of the reach of Almighty God, as they thought, they embraced another lover—SIN—and ignored the true God who demands obedience. But the Bible calls him a jealous God, a consuming fire. The cycle of reverential fear and spiritual indifference in the Old Testament story of Moses leading the children of Israel to the promised land graphically depicts the point. When their eyes and hearts were filled with an abiding awe and reverence for God there was no room for all the fear-dominating circumstances to control them. A heavenly perspective influenced by a reverential fear of God brings peace. A human perspective, with no consideration of God, brings pain.

This picture of God's awesome power continues into the New Testament. The book of Hebrews exhorted

Jewish Christians, "Therefore, since we are receiving a kingdom that cannot be shaken, let us be thankful, and so worship God acceptably with reverence and awe, for our God is a consuming fire" (Hebrews 12:28-29).

Consecrated fear is a heavenly perspective. One of God's prophets, Elijah, learned a lesson about God as a consuming fire when he entered a contest on Mount Carmel. His story also illustrates how easy it is for us to go from the thrill of victory, with a heavenly perspective, to the agony of defeat with a human perspective, all within a short time. Elijah had loudly challenged the idolatrous prophets of Baal to a contest between his Almighty God and their god Baal. The rules were that they would each prepare a bull for sacrifice, lay it on the wood on the altar, but not set fire to it. Instead, each side would call on their deity—Baal or the Lord God—to light the fire. Elijah let the prophets go first. He sat and watched all day as Baal's followers stood before their altar screaming, dancing, and even mutilating themselves to attract their god's attention. Every once in a while Elijah would taunt them, "Shout louder! Maybe Baal's asleep." Midday passed and they still "continued their frantic prophesying . . . but there was no response, no one answered, no one paid attention" (1 Kings 18:29).

Then it was Elijah's turn. Wanting the prophets of Baal to experience the persuasive power of the true God, Elijah built his altar, dug a trench around it large enough to hold water, arranged the wood and the sacrifice, then told them to pour water over the whole thing, so that "water ran down around the altar and even filled the trench" (verse 34). Now Elijah was ready to call on God to display His power. His confidence was at an all-time high, for he fully understood God and trusted in His faithfulness and awesome power.

"O LORD, God of Abraham, Isaac and Israel, let it be known today that you are God in Israel and that I am your servant and have done all these things at your command. Answer me, O LORD, answer me, so these people will know that you, O LORD, are God" (verses 36-37). Immediately "the fire of the LORD fell and burned up the sacrifice, the wood, the stones and the soil, and also licked up the water in the trench" (verse 38). Elijah's God was vindicated.

Cowardly fear results from a human perspective. Elijah had the blessed privilege of experiencing God's power protecting and providing for him when his perspective dramatically shifted from God to self. Shortly after the fire fell from heaven, Elijah had Baal's prophets killed. The infamous Queen Jezebel, who worshiped Baal, heard the news and sent word to Elijah, "May the gods deal with me, be it ever so severely, if by this time tomorrow I do not make your life like that of one of [Baal's prophets]" (1 Kings 19:2). Something about this threat to his life by one woman caused the prophet of faith to suddenly lose his divine perspective and fall into the clutches of fear. Elijah "ran for his life. When he came to Beersheba in Judah, he left his servant there, while he himself went a day's journey into the desert. He came to a broom tree, sat down under it and prayed that he might die. 'I have had enough, LORD,' he said. 'Take my life; I am no better than my ancestors'" (verse 4).

This man who courageously faced 450 prophets of Baal, seeing with his own eyes God's display of power, now sank into fear and depression because of the threats of one very wicked woman. The one who had pursued now retreated; the warrior who had destroyed God's enemies now wanted to die; the prophet of faith became faithless. The man of God, courageous on Carmel, cowered under a scraggly bush in the desert, trembling with fear. What caused Elijah to lose his trust in the omnipotent God, to change his perspective from God's power to his own weakness?

In this case, Elijah lost his perspective because he was physically and emotionally exhausted. He had neither slept nor eaten since before the contest. "He lay down under the tree and fell asleep" until an angel woke him and told him to eat the fresh bread waiting for him on a bed of hot coals and drink from a jar of water. This happened twice. It is sometimes possible to lose our perspective and concentrate on our own weaknesses instead of God's power when we are too tired or too hungry or too stressed to see circumstances through the filters of a heavenly perspective. But God is still strong, even when we are weak. He sent His angels to minister to His servant because He knew that Elijah trusted His unlimited power.

God's Protection Cultivates A Heavenly Perspective

Elisha, another of God's prophets, experienced Almighty God's protection. One of Israel's many enemies, Aram, was trying to set up a secret attack against Israel. But every time he got to the place where he had planned to set up camp, the Israelite army was there waiting for him. The enraged Aramean king questioned all of his officers, suspecting that one was a traitor. One of the men told the king about Elisha, a prophet of God, who knew all of the Arameans' plans before they were executed and revealed them to the king of Israel, even what Aram whispered in his bedroom.

The king found out that Elisha lived in Dothan. So he "sent horses and chariots and a strong force there. They went by night and surrounded the city" (2 Kings 6:14), hoping to destroy Elisha. The next morning Elisha's servant went outside and saw the army around the city. His perspective immediately locked on the terrifying circumstances; fear clenched his heart and his inner tape began to play, "Tomorrow could be a very bad day!" He must have felt like the little boy who portrayed Jesus walking on the Sea of Galilee in a church play. He was supposed to say, "It is I, be not afraid," but in the intensity of the dramatic moment, he cried, "It's me, and I'm scared!"

Elisha's servant ran to his master and asked, "Oh, my lord, what shall we do?" (verse 15). Elisha, however, was aware of another perspective. Even though the enemy was real, the army foreboding, and his servant's fears legitimate, Elisha was calm and confident. "Don't be afraid," the prophet told his servant, "those who are with us are more than those who are with them" (verse 16). Then he prayed, "O Lord, open his eyes so he may see." When the servant looked again, peering nervously between his fingers, the Aramean army was still there but he also "saw the hills full of horses and chariots of fire all around Elisha" (verse 17). God's army had been there all the time. All the servant needed was a faith-filled, heavenly perspective.

When our faith is stretched during fearful circumstances, sinful fear is supernaturally harnessed. Today Elisha's servant would break out in a contemporary refrain, "HE WAS THERE ALL THE TIME!"

Fear does not necessarily exaggerate an adverse situation, but it can cause us to misunderstand the circumstance. Like Elisha's servant, what our eyes see is only part of the picture; sight alone ignores the reality of God's presence and causes us to miss the major truths of His Word. Our duty—indeed, our privilege—is to trust God's promise that "those who are with us are more than those who are with them" in those fearful times when we are threatened by our circumstances.

God's Presence Cultivates A Heavenly Perspective

Earlier in the book we talked about the ten trembling spies who stood before Moses, defeated because of cowardice. These were ten of the twelve men who were sent into the Promised Land to spy on the enemy to ascertain their power. Only two of the spies, Joshua and Caleb, saw the situation through eyes of courage. They knew, as Moses told his people later, that the same God who "went ahead of you on your journey, in fire by night and in a cloud by day, to search out places for you to camp and to show you the way you should go" (Deuteronomy 1:33), would continue to be with them, carrying them "as a father carries his son, all the way" (verse 31).

These two trusting men saw the same dangers as the ten, a land that "devours those living in it," popu-lated with people "of great size" (Numbers 13:32). But they filtered their fearful thoughts through God's promised presence and were able to give a positive report. The ten saw only the giants, their fears obstruct-ing a vision of God's unfailing promise to be with them.

As we know, the result of seeing the obstacles through the eyes of trust in God's guidance was that these two men were the only ones to go into the land God had promised them.

My younger brother Ted is a Lt. Colonel in the U.S. Army. He serves as a Chaplain and was in the midst of the Desert Storm conflict. He was personally keenly aware of God's presence. His confidence and faith was contagious. His proclamation of trust in God's presence to the troops who would be in combat the next morning resulted in many committing their lives to Christ through faith. Colonel Nichols had the great privilege of baptizing many of the troops who put their trust in God's personal presence in the midst of life-threatening, fear-generating circumstances.

God's Plan Cultivates A Heavenly Perspective

A World War II bomber was completing its final bombing raid. The crew had experienced remarkable success and needed to make only one more flight before they would be relieved of the bombing assignment. As they taxied to the runway, they received the thumbs up sign and a salute from the commander of the air-base. Penetration into enemy skies once again led to a successful bombing mission. On their return flight, amid joyous celebration, an unusually strong tailwind caused them to reach their landing zone a full twenty-five minutes early. According to their navigation system, it was time to land. However, a hurried conference over the intercom impelled them to trust their intuitive judgment and previous experiences, so they continued the flight. As a result, they overran the landing site and ran out of fuel.

A diary, found at the crash site, detailed the conflict: should we trust our judgment or the trustworthiness of the navigation system that has been so faithful during previous flights?

When we are dealing with the tempests of fear and storms of uncertainty, we too need to fix our eyes on the Divine Navigation System, not on our own knowledge and experience in handling the turbulences of life.

Often the stressors of life cause us to be distracted from God's perfect plan. We trust our own intuitive or experiential judgment and the results can be serious. Thank God for His wonderful plan, His Living Word. He truly has provided for us a Divine Navigation System that will never fail. "Let us fix our eyes on Jesus, the author and perfecter of our faith" (Hebrews 12:2).

PERSONAL EVALUATION

1. I can think of at least one time when a fearful situation was provoked and exaggerated by my human perspective. It was when . . .

My perspective is generally more characterized by:
   (a) fear
   (b) faith

2. I remember a specific time when my perspective dramatically changed during a fearful situation (like Elisha's servant) with new inspiration or spiritual insight. It was when . . .

3. As I think back over this chapter, I realize that I need to create a more consistent heavenly perspective by developing greater faith in (circle one):
   (a) God's power
   (b) God's protection
   (c) God's presence
   (d) God's plan
I selected this particular one because . . .

PRACTICAL APPLICATION

1. Make a point every day to pray the following prayer so that God can help you adjust your perspective: "Lord Jesus, open my eyes to see better Your power, protection, presence, and plan. Thank You for Your promises."

2. Write down one thing that is troubling you right now. Now see how you can adjust your perspective of the problem by seeing it through the eyes of God's power, protection, presence, or plan.

3. Memorize Jeremiah 33:3: "Call to me and I will answer you and tell you great and unsearchable things you do not know."

PRAYERFUL MEDITATION

1. FEAR NOT—We have freedom to see the fear-inducing challenges of life from a heavenly perspective.

"Therefore we will not fear, though the earth give way and the mountains fall into the heart of the sea, though its waters roar and foam and the mountains quake with their surging."
—Psalm 46:2

2. FEAR NOT—I will trust God and not fear what man can do to me.

"In God, whose word I praise, in God I trust; I will not be afraid. What can mortal man do to me?"
—Psalm 56:4

3. FEAR NOT—God's Word provides confidence and will help us rest and sleep.

"When you lie down, you will not be afraid; when you lie down, your sleep will be sweet. Have no fear of sudden disaster or of the ruin that overtakes the wicked, for the LORD will be your confidence and will keep your foot from being snared."
—Proverbs 3:24-26

chapter

Trust God's Faithfulness

The second powerful priority in learning how to harness fear is trusting God's absolute faithfulness, especially when dealing with fearful times. Absolute trust is easier to talk about than to experience and express.

"The huge crowd of people were watching the famous tightrope walker, Blondin, cross Niagara Falls one day. Blondin crossed the rope numerous times—a 1,000 foot trip, 160 feet above the raging water. The story is told that he spoke to the crowd, asking if they believed he could take one of them across. Of course, they all gave their enthusiastic assent. Then he approached a man and asked him to get on his back and go with him. The man who was invited refused to go."[1] When we are faced with fear-saturated situations we must fully trust God and demonstrate that trust through our actions. Mental assent, or even verbal assent, is not enough. There must be trust in Christ alone. We must place ourselves in His loving arms.

Situations that provoke fear within us are woven into the very fabric of our lives. While many people in the world face more fearful situations with more frequency than we do in the United States, fear-filled experiences still touch all of us, either directly or through the trials of others. These fear-generating circumstances all test our faith in God's absolute faithfulness. "Where is God? Why does He let these things happen?"

The "fear-not" verses in the Bible suggest a distinct relationship between fear and faith. Jesus often asked His followers, "Why are you so afraid? Have you no faith?" Our faith is a direct outflow of our belief and trust in God's absolute faithfulness. In this chapter we will talk about the priority of God's faithfulness as a foundation upon which we can cultivate our own personal/spiritual faith, to be discussed in the next chapter. The lethal capacity of threats to our well-being, even as we lean on the mother-hen protection of faith in God, still grips our hearts. We all need to go through the workshop "Fear and Faith 101." Fear-drenched situations in life provide great opportunities for being stretched in our trust in God's faithfulness. Fear literally magnifies our sensitivity to and appreciation for our faithful God.

While facing fear/fear-not situations, those of us who believe in and trust God have learned to lean on His promise to be with us in all things. We turn our eyes upward and speak the name of Jesus to feel God's strong hand on our shoulder. Our trust in God's faithfulness is precious to Him because, as Peter says in his first letter, even "though now for a little while you may have had to suffer grief in all kinds of trials" brought about by the Adversary, our own foolishness, or the consequences of a no longer perfect world, God will always be at our side to provide protection, comfort, and the opportunity to exercise our faith in Him. Trials,

Peter says, come "so that your faith . . . may be proved genuine and may result in praise, glory and honor when Jesus Christ is revealed" (1 Peter 1:6-7).

A small boy, shopping with his father in a discount warehouse, wanders away from his dad, staring in wonder at the tall shelves, big boxes, and bright lights. Suddenly a forklift backs across the aisle, beeping insistently. The child looks around him quickly. "Where's Dad?" Just then, the big, familiar hand rests on his shoulder, and the little boy loses his fear. "Hi, Dad, I knew you were there all the time; I just couldn't see you at first."

Like this small boy, frightening situations that temporarily distract us from our heavenly Father's presence may panic us at first. But, if we have regularly exercised our faith in God's faithfulness, we quickly look up and say with great relief, "Dear Lord, I knew you were there all the time."

Fear issues a wake-up call in those of us who trust God, reminding us of our constant need of Him and that He is with us and cares for us. "Trust in him at all times, O people; pour out your hearts to him, for God is our refuge" (Psalm 62:8).

Trust God's Faithfulness In Times of Testing

While Job's tenacious trust in God's faithfulness is puzzling to many, to some of us it is a challenge. His statement, "Though he slay me, yet will I hope in Him" (Job 13:15), covers a long trek down fear's path. Job had already lost his possessions and his children when Satan shot his final flaming arrow, stripping him of his health. Job's wife then turned on him and cruelly slashed at him, "Are you still holding on to your integrity? Curse God and die!" Job retorted, "You are talking like a foolish woman. Shall we accept good

from God, and not trouble?" (Job 2:9-10). His reply
revealed his unwavering focus on God's faithfulness
which kept him from apostasy. He did, however, do a
lion's share of complaining, for which he was aptly
rebuked (Job 38 to 41).

Job believed in God's faithfulness because he knew
that God was trustworthy. Even if God never delivered him from all his woes, Job knew that he could
trust God's wisdom, love, and will. This trust in God
protected Job against such foes as depression (Job 3),
bitterness (Job 7), and fear (Job 13:21).

Job's consolation in times of unrelenting pain and
confusion was that he had not denied the words of
the Holy One (Job 6:10). He looked beyond the present agony to his future bliss in the resurrection (Job
19:25-26).

I will never forget the moment Pastor Jeremiah
asked me to come to his office for a meeting. As I
walked into the room, the atmosphere was quite
sober. I was immediately aware that his agenda for this
special meeting was very serious. As I sat down the
Pastor said, "Ken, I have some very disturbing news
to share with you. I just returned from the doctor and
he confirmed that I have cancer." We both began to
cry and just sat silently for a short time. I was really
shocked by the news. We prayed together and then
immediately began to develop a plan on how to handle the news with his family, friends, and the ministry
family. In addition, we developed a plan for the best
treatment available and consulted one of our dear
medical friends, Dr. Marvin Eastlund. There was a period of weeks that the Pastor and I would deal with our
natural fears by reminding ourselves of God's faithfulness. The sobering reality of our infirmities creates an
environment for intense fears to develop.

Pastor Jeremiah has been through two surgeries
since that time and his cancer has been declared to be

in complete remission. The Pastor responded to his life-threatening challenge with a gradual growth of faith, hope and love. His faith has increased, his anticipation of God's provision was apparent and his love for friends and family was experienced at an even greater depth. It was refreshingly obvious to me that this man who has faithfully preached faith, hope, and love for so many years was being re-created in the image of God as a direct result of his response of trusting in times of testing. His journey from living in fear to living by faith has been a great testimony to his family, friends, church, and to the thousands who listen to the Turning Point radio program around the world. Visits to the doctor for a check-up are not without fearful challenges. But his personal testimony affirms that he has been wonderfully stretched in his trust in God's faithfulness—even when facing a life-threatening illness.

Trust God's Faithfulness In Times of Terror

The power of natural phenomena—a hurricane that leaves a path of destruction through Hawaii, an earthquake that takes a heavy toll in Kobe, a tornado that cuts a swath of terror through a small town in Michigan, or a terrorist attack such as that in Oklahoma City—often sneak up on our blind side. If we have exercised our trust in God, we will be better prepared to cope with these times of terror.

Air Force Captain Scott O'Grady was prepared. He experienced nearly constant terror for six days while armed men searched for him, some coming within three to five feet of him as he lay motionless with his face in the dirt, covered with mud and leaves. He had ejected from his flaming F-16 when the fighter was hit by an SA-6 surface-to-air missile fired from a Bosnian-

Serb stronghold. As he floated toward earth he could
see men below him, waiting for him to land. When he
hit the ground he took only seconds to get out of his
parachute and hide from those intent on taking him
prisoner. He said of those six days, "For the most part,
my face was in the dirt, and I was just praying they
wouldn't see me or hear me." One time he lay
motionless, as a cow with a herder nearby grazed on
grass between his legs. After his dramatic rescue by
U.S. marines he said that he always felt the prayers of
the people back home. He also prayed for himself: "I
prayed to God and asked Him for a lot of things, and
He delivered throughout the entire time." He said that
when he prayed for rain, God gave him rain. When
he prayed, "Lord, let me at least have someone know
I'm alive and maybe come rescue me," that night
another pilot heard his radio call for help. Scott said
he wasn't a hero; he was just a scared little bunny
rabbit, but he trusted God's faithfulness throughout
the time of terror.[2]

God is still the Master of nature, the Mighty God,
the Prince of Peace, the Ruler from sea to sea, the
Sovereign Supreme Being, the Head of the Church,
the King of kings and Lord of lords. His care for us is
as constant as the rolling tide. Our fears matter to
Him. Once we understand that He cares and main-
tains complete control and has limitless ability to meet
our every need, we can relax, and our controlling
fears will evaporate like hot steam rising into the air.

I have not been exposed to many situations that
truly created a sense of terror. But I recall very clearly
an occasion when I had absolutely no control over a
circumstance that was filled with fright. I took my
younger daughter Kara to a carnival and we were
having a great time together. I persuaded her to go on
a very scary ride with me. She was resistant but the
macho part of her dad persisted. We got on the

upside down ride and it was absolutely terror-filled. She was barely big enough and she began to slide around in the seat. I was holding my screaming child with one hand and the safety bar with the other. I screamed, yelled and did everything I could to get the operator's attention. Finally, he detected the serious-ness of our situation and stopped the ride. Kara and I were both traumatized by the few seconds of terror. Now, I don't remember praying out loud—I was too busy screaming at the operator, but I do remember being conscious of my desperate need for God's help to keep us from being hurt. Kara teasingly reminds me from time to time how I have scarred her for life with this terror-filled childhood drama.

God was on the Sea of Galilee that frightful night when the disciples went through the workshop on fear and faith. Their learning lab out in the midst of a stormy sea not only exposed the depth of their terror but also the shallowness of their faith. They did not do as well as Job did in the course, but the experi-ence added a little more to their trust in God's faith-fulness. Jesus knew that they would have to go through far greater terrors than a raging sea: "You must be on your guard. You will be handed over to the local councils and flogged in the synagogues. . . . All men will hate you because of me, but he who stands firm to the end will be saved" (Mark 13:9, 13). They had to begin to build their absolute trust in God's faithfulness, regardless of how awful or fearful the circumstances.

Although our voyage through life may never take us into enemy territory in a foreign land, as Scott's did, or place us in the disciples' boat, each of us will have our date with personal terror. Our knee-jerk reaction is often the same as the disciples in the storm: panic! But if we listen closely, we will hear the Holy Spirit of God whisper, "You of little faith, why are you so afraid?" He will tell us to be still, to rest and trust in His faithful care.

Trust God's Faithfulness During Political Upheaval

Alarms trumpeted by various news media of political changes also invoke fear in our minds and hearts. Media speculation about retirement benefits being frozen, taxes being raised, health care undergoing a major overhaul, and news of outrages against human rights, military coups overtaking a nation, and wars and rumors of wars cause us to ask, "Does God know what's going on? Does He care?" While we rejoice to see Russia open her arms to Christian values, invite people to teach the Bible in her schools, and encourage greater freedoms, we are increasingly being denied these privileges in our own country: less freedom, decaying moral values, an ongoing holocaust against the unborn child, unbridled sexual perversity. Even as we anticipate the "golden years," the cold-blooded term "euthanasia" causes a shiver of fear to shoot through our veins. One cartoon depicted a bride and groom at the altar with the man saying, "Till euthanasia do us part." Loss of control over moral standards which we believe God's Word teaches, generates a sense of pandemonium, accompanied by fear.

One of the newsletters from Dr. James Dobson's organization, *Focus on the Family*, details the first five executive decisions signed by our current president, which all run contrary to family and Christian values: (1) That fetal tissue from aborted babies can be used for medical research. (2) That RU46 be approved as an acceptable method of abortion in the United States. (3) That counseling is no longer required prior to abortions. (4) That the government seriously question the ban on homosexuals in the military. (5) That federal funding for abortions be approved.

Many other religious leaders are sounding the alarm that we are rapidly approaching the kind of one-world government that will herald in the rise to power of the Antichrist, as prophesied in Scripture. These fearful changes in the political status quo should act as warnings to us not to panic but to take advantage of another opportunity to increase our faith in God's faithfulness.

As much as it is in our power we should, of course, do what we can to halt anything that threatens our country or our families by voicing our concern through letters to our representatives and in the voting booth. But worry and fear cannot impact the reality of a changing society. One author refers to worry as a rocking chair: it gives us something to do but doesn't get us anywhere. The only hope that will change the world is the One who changes men's hearts—Jesus Christ.

Fred came to the ALIVE counseling center for help. He was experiencing such enormous fears and anxiety that he had to quit his job. He believed that political changes would have a profound negative impact on his business, his retirement, his children's future, and his Christian values. Fred was severely upset about political movements outside his direct control or significant influence. He became obsessed with media descriptions of dire changes. His emotional frenzy was rooted in his obsession with real and imagined negative political consequences, coupled with a feeling of helplessness.

The Apostle Paul told Christians in Rome:

> Everyone must submit himself to the governing authorities, for there is no authority except that which God has established. The authorities that exist have been established by God. Consequently, he who rebels against the authority is rebelling

against what God has instituted, and those who
do so will bring judgment on themselves. For
rulers hold no terror for those who do right, but
for those who do wrong. Do you want to be free
from fear of the one in authority? Then do what is
right and he will commend you (Romans 13:1-3).

This admonition does not distinguish between
moral or immoral leaders; politicians cannot affect
what goes on in our own hearts. Nor can they stop
God from exercising His great power and protection
over His own.

With much counseling, Fred began to regain his
emotional and spiritual balance. He did so, primarily,
by answering fear's relentless pursuit with faith in
God's sovereign control over the nation; in God's sure
reward, both here and in the hereafter; and in God's
children's efforts to fly the banner of morality and
social justice. Christians must work diligently for the
cause of righteousness, but reckon with the reality
that God's judgment on an immoral nation may come
in the form of servitude to leaders who sometimes
unknowingly champion the cause of the Adversary.
God will be faithful to each of us and to our nation.
The psalmist said, "It is God who judges: He brings
one down, he exalts another" (Psalm 75:7). God's
faithfulness stands independent of the outcome of
life's fearful political situations.

Trust God's Faithfulness Even When Things Don't End Well

Even while radio and TV evangelists boom the
errant gospel of health, wealth, and prosperity, each
of us who has enlisted as a soldier of the King of
kings should be prepared to join the fear and faith-
filled chorus of Shadrach, Meshach, and Abednego.

After refusing to worship Nebuchadnezzar's golden image, they were sentenced to a furnace of blazing fire. As they were propelled toward the fire, King Nebuchadnezzar shot this question at them: "What god will be able to rescue you from my hand?" The men replied, "O Nebuchadnezzar, we do not need to defend ourselves before you in this matter. If we are thrown into the blazing furnace, the God we serve is able to save us from it, and he will rescue us from your hand, O king. But even if he does not, we want you to know, O king, that we will not serve your gods or worship the image of gold you have set up" (Daniel 3:15-18).

Greg and Barbara Meeks know what it is like to trust in God's faithfulness even when from a human perspective things don't end well. Greg, an ordained minister, and Barbara, a children/youth director, had believed in and taught God's healing power for many years. When their daughter, twelve-year-old Christen, was diagnosed as having cancer they just knew that God would heal her. Their church and many friends and neighbors prayed regularly for Christen's healing, believing that God would come through for them. But two weeks before her fifteenth birthday, Christen died. At her funeral, many of her high school friends heard the gospel and her parents' testimony that now Christen knew the ultimate healing because she was in heaven where she could no longer be touched by pain and illness. Greg, Barbara, Christen, and her younger brother Isaac had fully trusted in God during the years of chemotherapy and other treatment. Their faith in God's faithfulness was truly tested to the limit. As you can imagine, this family's faith in God's faithfulness during this very difficult time had a profound impact on both youth and adults in their small community.

Many are eager to give testimony of how God wonderfully provided for them when they had a great need, or delivered them from a fiery furnace. As God reminded Jeremiah, "I am the LORD, the God of all mankind. Is anything too hard for me?" (Jeremiah 32:27). Nothing is too hard for God. We joyfully point to His salvation, praise His name for answered prayer, and proclaim His faithfulness. And well we should. Not one of us should ever walk in cadence with the nine lepers who failed to thank Jesus for His healing. But the greatest test of trust in God's faithfulness is how we respond when lions tear us limb from limb, and when the final chapter of adversity does not have a storybook ending.

If we trust in God's faithfulness to sustain us, develop us, calm us, use us, and eventually bring us home to be with Him, we also need to trust His faithfulness when fearful circumstances do not bring a happy ending. Christians are not exempt from the reality of terminal disease, the ravages of drought, earthquakes and floods, the effects of budget cuts and joblessness, and threats of religious or political persecution.

Hebrews 11 chronicles those followers of God who escaped harm and who were raised from the dead. But it also tells about the others who "were tortured and refused to be released, so that they might gain a better resurrection. Some faced jeers and flogging, while still others were chained and put in prison. They were stoned; they were sawed in two; they were put to death by the sword. They went about in sheepskins and goatskins, destitute, persecuted and mistreated . . . they wandered in deserts and mountains and in caves and holes in the ground" (verses 35-38). Through it all, they persisted in trusting the faithfulness of God; with the strength of God's adequacy they battled the inborn fears that attended their suffering.

We need to cultivate daily reminders of the absolute faithfulness of God. In good times and bad, in success and failure, God is faithful. When we focus on His faithfulness in our behalf, we will be released from the bondage of fear.

It is very difficult, while cowering beneath a burden of fear, to have faith in God's faithfulness. But if, once we have dumped the fear-filled load, we take time to look back at the experience, we will see how the tender shoots of our growing faith were protected and nurtured by the greenhouse of God's faithfulness. To put it another way, if we flex our feeble faith muscles as we enter the ring to spar with fear, then flex them again at the final bell, we will see tangible growth.

There is a true story told of a farmer who had a very young son. The farmer was carrying a large and heavy basket, and his son wanted to help him. The farmer cut a large stick and placed it through the handle of the basket so that the end toward himself was very short, while the end toward the son was three or four times as long. Each took hold of his end of the stick, and the basket was lifted and carried easily. The son bore the burden with his father. But the child found his work easy and his burden light because his father assumed the heavier end of the load. So it is when we are confronted with the realities of our inadequacies, insecurities, and infirmities. We must remember that we are wonderfully yoked together with Jesus Christ, who will carry the weight of fear-generating circumstances which exceed our human abilities. You can absolutely trust God's faithfulness in your behalf!

Matthew 11:28 says: "Come to me, all you who are weary and burdened, and I will give you rest. Take my yoke upon you and learn from me, for I am gentle and humble in heart, and you will find rest for your souls."

PERSONAL EVALUATION

1. I have a habit of not expecting success. Right now I am going to change my attitude about one issue that troubles me. That is . . .

2. God has provided for me and stayed close to me in past circumstances. Some of these were:

3. I will tap into God's power today because I am fearful about a future event. That event is . . .

I am going to rest in the promises of God and let Him encourage me.

PRACTICAL APPLICATION

1. Memorize 2 Corinthians 4:18: "So we fix our eyes not on what is seen, but on what is unseen. For what is seen is temporary, but what is unseen is eternal."

2. This week try to focus on one specific aspect of God's faithfulness, for example His faithfulness in times of testing. Write out the specific aspect and under it include one or two personal or Biblical examples of this aspect of God's nature that come to mind.

3. Take the initials of your full name and write down something about God's faithfulness that begins with each letter. For example, my name is Ken so I could start my project with the letter K. God's faithfulness is obvious in how He provides the Knowledge we need to successfully live for Him.

PRAYERFUL MEDITATION

1. FEAR NOT—God is with you during times of terror and confusion.

"You will not fear the terror of night, nor the arrow that flies by day, nor the pestilence that stalks in darkness, nor the plague that destroys at midday."   —Psalm 91:5-6

2. FEAR NOT—God is with you when you are tested and tried for your faith.

"Peace I leave with you; my peace I give you. I do not give to you as the world gives. Do not let your hearts be troubled and do not be afraid."
                                            —John 14:27

3. FEAR NOT—God is looking at the long view, your eternal destiny.

"Do not be afraid of what you are about to suffer. I tell you, the devil will put some of you in prison, to test you, and you will suffer persecution for ten days. Be faithful, even to the point of death, and I will give you the crown of life."
                                    —Revelation 2:10

Notes:
[1]   Kennedy, D. James. *Evangelism Explosion.* Fort Lauderdale: Coral Ridge Presbyterian Church, 1977: 108.
[2]   Fedarko, Kevin & Thompson, Mark. "All for One," *Time.* 19 June 1995: 21-23.

chapter

Faith That Perseveres

A nd now these three remain: faith, hope and love" (1 Corinthians 13:13).

So far we have discussed two foundation principles in the Biblical plan and spiritual process of harnessing the incredible power of fear: (1) cultivating a heavenly perspective, and (2) understanding God's absolute faithfulness. In this and the next two chapters we will flesh out the discussion on solutions focusing on three of the highest priorities in spiritual growth.

When the Apostle Paul introduced 1 Corinthians 13, which is often called, the Love Chapter, he began with, "I will show you the most excellent way" (1 Corinthians 12:31), which is the way of love. When he ended the Love Chapter he said, "And now these three remain: faith, hope and love." The first of these— faith, and how it helps you to harness fear—is what we want to talk about in this chapter.

This verse about faith, hope, and love comes in the middle of Paul's admonition about spiritual gifts. The church in Corinth was evidently having a problem with their gifts of the Spirit. Perhaps they were beginning to compare their gifts, measuring one against another, trying to determine which gift was more important. Paul's word to them was that "God has arranged the parts in the body, every one of them, just as he wanted them to be" (1 Corinthians 12:18). Their individual gifts combined to build up their local body, their church, "for the common good" (v. 7).

Developing these priorities literally makes it impossible for fear to become the controlling master of your mind, emotions and life. These spiritual qualities leave no room in your heart for a controlling, sinful fear.

Marlene, Kara, and I traveled to New York City for a few days of sightseeing after I presented a seminar in Pennsylvania. It was Kara's first visit to the big city, so we tried to see as much as possible in our brief stay. The rush, the crowds, and the noise were a little intimidating for us. The strange and unfamiliar atmosphere plus the many unkempt, lounging individuals kept us careful and alert, especially since it was Kara's first time on a subway.

But Marlene had a brief time to respond to fear with an exercise in faith. We were rushing to get uptown, had purchased our subway tokens, and Kara and I quickly pushed through the turnstile. We jumped on the subway only to look back to see that Marlene's token was stuck and she couldn't get through. We shall never forget the look on her face as she watched us disappear down the tracks. Believe me, her first response as depicted on her countenance was not faith—it was fear. She stepped back into the waiting area and I was keenly aware of how lonely and scared she felt. Thankfully we had just discussed with the man in the ticket booth where we should get off to go to Central Park and Broadway.

In her purse Marlene always carries a miniature Bible that has one verse from every book in the Bible. For comfort, she decided to start reading in Genesis to pass the time waiting for the next train. Her heart was comforted and her fear subsided. She pointed out that the verse for Esther read, "I go in unto the king . . . and if I perish, I perish." She boarded the next train, and got off at our prearranged stop where Kara and I anxiously waited to be reunited with her.

The author of the book of Hebrews describes faith in this way: "Now faith is being sure of what we hope for and certain of what we do not see" (Hebrews 11:1). This kind of faith is different from that which we spoke of in the previous chapter. Then we talked about God's faithfulness; in this chapter we talk about the kind of faith we can build up only by exercising it, just as we build up muscles by exercising them. The "little faith" Jesus accused His followers of having in Matthew 8:26 ("You of little faith, why are you so afraid?") needed to develop muscle and grow into the "great faith" He commended in Matthew 8:10: "I tell you the truth, I have not found anyone in Israel with such great faith."

Chesty Puller's admonition "No pain, no gain" holds true spiritually as well as physically. Spiritual pain is what you may feel when you exercise your faith in times of fear-filled trials. Your Sovereign God allows these fearful times because they will build onto your faith. Great faith is always born out of great challenges, especially fear-filled challenges that require perseverance. Max Lucado zeros in on this concept in his book *The Eye of the Storm* when he writes: "Biographies of bold disciples begin with chapters of honest terror. Fear of death. Fear of failure. Fear of loneliness. Fear of a wasted life. Faith begins when you see God on the mountain and you are in the valley and you know that you're too weak to make the climb. You see what you need . . . you see what you have . . . and it isn't enough . . . but He is . . . *Faith that begins with fear will end up nearer the Father.*"[1] (Emphasis added)

Trials Are a Fact of Life

James begins his epistle talking about the trials the followers of Jesus would encounter because they lived in an unbelieving world: "Consider it pure joy, my brothers, whenever you face trials of many kinds, because you know that the testing of your faith develops perseverance. Perseverance must finish its work so that you may be mature and complete, not lacking anything" (James 1:2-4). In these few verses James tells us why we need faith that won't quit in the face of fear. First, trials are a fact of life; second, faith perseveres under trial; third, faith provides courage to go on; fourth, you build faith by fixing your eyes on Jesus. Perseverance is when your hands and feet keep on working when your head says it can't be done.

At the beginning of this book I talked about how the Adversary entraps people with a preoccupation with their pains and problems of the past, causing them to be paranoid about the future, and creating paralysis in the present. That was Pat McIntosh's personal tragedy. Pat and her husband, Dave, told my crisis counseling class at Moody Bible Institute Graduate School all about it. Pat told of years of sexual and psychological abuse.

These two kept the class intently focused for nearly two hours, without a break, by sharing their journey from fear to faith.

All her life, Pat's journey was manipulated by fears that were tied to the pain of her past. She was a prisoner, locked up, afraid to feel, refusing to be vulnerable in relationships, afraid to trust, unable to face the

truth of her painful past. Her controlling fears contributed to a severe faith deficiency.

Through godly counsel over an extended period of
time, Pat has dealt with much of her painful past and
now gives testimony of a deep relationship with her
faithful God. Faith in God's power and presence did
not remove the disgusting abuse, but it supplied her
with courage to face her fears, trust God's faithfulness,
and increase her faith. She carefully includes in her
testimony the teamwork that made the difference: her
faithful husband, a supportive family, genuine friends,
a loving church, competent counselors, and, most
importantly, the wonderful Word of God and the precious ministry of the Holy Spirit. When the McIntoshes
are finished with their session at Moody, students
obviously envy Pat's intimacy with God.

Pat knows firsthand what it is like to be intimidated
and terrified by abusers and then be subjugated to
fear throughout much of her adult life. But while giving her testimony, she glows with God's grace
because she also knows what it is like to be set free.
None of us envy her journey but we all recognize that
a wounded heart, manipulated for years by fear, is
now saturated with God's grace and love. Her growing confidence in God's faithfulness (despite the awful
childhood abuse) and her courageous faith are
dynamic contributors to her being set free from a lifestyle dominated by fear.

Faith Perseveres Under Trial

After telling his readers that they would endure
"many kinds" of trials, James mentions some of them.
Then he goes on to tell how they, and we, can persevere in the face of them. James's letter is directed to
the "twelve tribes" that were "scattered among the
nations," scattered in an effort to escape persecution
because of their faith in God. We may never have to

encounter the same kinds of trials these early followers of Jesus did, but we still are faced with problems
that create fear in our hearts. Some of the things
James talks about which we also face are financial
lack, temptations, physical affliction, and sometimes
social injustice. We may not suffer physical persecution as they did, but the Adversary knows how to
bring us trials that cause deep fear. But, as James said,
these trials are designed to make us stronger believers. Various trials come, faith is tested, patience is
developed, and maturity is the result. The following
illustration captures the essence of how the faith-filled
struggle with fear-drenched situations has the potential
to create great strength.

Every fall the monarch caterpillar crawls to the end
of a twig, fashions a meticulously fabricated cocoon
around itself, slams the door and goes to sleep for the
winter. The following spring something utterly miraculous happens—out struggles a beautiful monarch butterfly. If we were to walk past the cocoon just as the
butterfly chooses to emerge from its magic chamber,
we would see a fierce struggle going on. Perhaps we
would be tempted to help the emerging insect as it
pushes, pulls, and wiggles its way out, sometimes
falling back in complete exhaustion. We might feel
that we should take some tweezers and pull back the
opening ever so slightly in order to free the butterfly
from its potential coffin.

Well-meaning though such a gesture would be, it
would seal the butterfly's doom. For the very struggle
to break from the cocoon strengthens its wings so that
they are strong enough to fly. If the butterfly does not
struggle to get out, it will be condemned to crawl
among the twigs. Unable to fly, it will starve to death
or become dinner for a neighboring bird. Prerequisites
for transforming the ugly little caterpillar into a beautiful butterfly are time in the cocoon and the energy-

demanding trial of struggling to get out.

Much like the monarch butterfly, our ultimate beauty and final form are directly influenced by the fear-filled experiences we struggle with in our lives. So, when we face a major challenge, will we be paralyzed by fear or stretched in faith? Every promise of God should keep us standing firm, not cowering, filled with faith.

Perhaps you can see more clearly the priority of a faith-filled perseverance through the following stories. A T-shirt may read, "I'm Proud to be a Marine," but it would take an entire fabric shop to hold the full message that would begin, "I left mom and dad one morning at the bus station. I rode on with visions of patriotism, posters, and promises. The barracks looked okay until I was awakened three hours before I expected to get up. Then I was called names—names I had heard before, but only when I had a chance to fight back. We lined up, ran out, and climbed over obstacles until I groaned, 'I can't do this.' But I did. I survived. I feel strong. And I'm proud to be a Marine."

I can remember with considerable clarity and emotion the rigorous weeks of training. The beginning class of potential paratroopers starts with commitment, enthusiasm, and a large measure of fear. But the drill sergeant (looking for a few good men) makes life so tough that a third of the class drops out before reaching the finish line. I will never erase from my memory doing push-ups with the sergeant lying on the ground, face to face with me, yelling, "Have you had enough soldier?"

"No, sergeant!" (I lied)

"Then give me fifty more." Experience had taught me to expect it. The high drop-out rate was largely attributed to constant intimidation, forcing the recruit to exceed his emotional and physical tolerance threshold.

Our spiritual battle with fear is much like this. The Adversary is like the drill sergeant, putting on the pressure, marketing fear, and then at our weakest moment inviting us to abandon our goal. But his reasons are not to strengthen and equip us for life's battles, but to defeat us. He cannot strip us of our eternal security in Christ, but he hopes to make quitters out of us, spiritual warfare casualties. And he delights in our defeat. However, "The testing of your faith develops perseverance. Perseverance must finish its work so that you may be *mature and complete, not lacking anything"* (James 1:3-4, italics added).

Faith Provides the Courage to Go On

It seems that the greater the challenge, the greater the opportunity for genuine growth. Extracting all the spiritual value from a trial is like grabbing an orange half, thrusting it down upon the juicer, then pressing and turning for all you're worth. The intense effort extracts every drop of juice from the orange. Then, once you pick out all the seeds, you have the satisfaction of pouring that tasty nectar into a glass and drinking it down. In a sense, the more intense your efforts, the more fruitful and refreshing the results.

There is a direct relationship between the intensity of the trial and the potential for increased faith. Before deciding on taking the climb, many of the 300,000 people who ascend Mount Fuji each year stop to consider the challenge of a nine- to sixteen-mile climb (add another three to five miles for slippage on loose ash). With some apprehension, they read about the route up the mountain (paying close attention to rest stops). Then they begin to prepare their bodies for the strain before they fly to Japan. They walk during their lunch hours and climb mountains near their homes on weekends. But the price they have to pay for the experience seems small when they anticipate the sunrise greeting them in reward for their all-night climb. They can just see their "I climbed Mount Fuji" T-shirt and savor recording the event on their calendars.

When the big day arrives they stand at the foot of Fuji, trying to see the top in the dark. Then, step by step, they begin the steep climb, feeling their way, slipping on volcanic ash. As they conquer the last summit, the sunrise and T-shirt and sense of achievement become reality. They return home holding their heads a little higher, standing a little taller, stepping a little lighter because their confidence has grown. After all, they climbed Fuji! Having the courage/faith to conquer fearful challenges sweetens the reward when the task is completed.

There is a direct relationship between the price paid and delight in a job well done, especially when the challenge is fear-filled, requiring courage and faith—coping with fear, paying the price, and finishing the course. That's faith-generated perseverance when facing fear-generating challenges in life.

Fear tempts us to quit when the going gets tough, but faith supplies the courage to endure hardships and trials. When fear entices you to quit, soldier of Christ, don't! Never stop anticipating the joy of standing before our heavenly Commander and having Him place on our heads the crown of life for faith in fearful times.

It was recorded as the shortest commencement speech in history. This special speaker, who had been pursued for years by the prestigious universities, finally accepted an invitation extended by his former grade school, Harrow, where he had been in the lower third of his class and showed little potential. However, he graduated and went on to the university. Now he was invited back to speak to the graduates. After all the preliminaries, he moved slowly to the lectern, paused, cleared his throat and spoke these words: "Young gentlemen, never give in! Never give in! Never, never, never. Never—in anything great or small, large or petty—never give in except to convic-

tions of honor and good sense." He then returned to
the comfortable chair on the platform and sat down.
The crowd, at first stunned into silence, spontaneously
leaped to their feet and delivered a standing ovation
that lasted for many minutes! They understood what Sir
Winston Churchill was communicating to the graduates.

At a time in which the world faced some of the
most fearful circumstances in history, Churchill issued
messages of hope, faith, and determination. His words
of inspiration struck a greater blow to the enemy than
any navy destroyer could have done. His fears were
legitimate, but his persevering faith was contagious.

A friend of mine since childhood, Mr. O.B. Scott,
has had to learn many of life's toughest lessons. No
doubt the most difficult was the loss of his lovely wife
to cancer. In more recent years he has faced multiple
physical problems, but he has always faced his fears
with a remarkable sense of confidence. He sent me
this poem, not only to encourage me but to minister
to others who are enduring times of adversity:

When things go wrong, as they sometimes will,
When the road you're trudging seems all uphill,
When the funds are low and the debts are high,
And you want to smile, but you have to sigh,
When care is pressing you down a bit,
Rest if you must, but don't you quit.
Life is queer with its twists and turns,
As every one of us sometimes learns,
And many a person turns about
When they might have won had they stuck it out.
Don't give up though the pace seems slow,
You may succeed with another blow.
Often the struggler has given up,
When he might have captured the victor's cup;
And he learned too late when the night came down,
How close he was to the golden crown.

Success is failure turned inside out,
The silver tint of the clouds of doubt,
So stick to the fight when you're hardest hit,
It's when things seem worst that you mustn't quit.
Author unknown

God promises and abundantly provides challenges in life that are loving opportunities to overcome fear by developing greater faith.

PERSONAL EVALUATION

1. What one event or situation this past year was my most "faith-stretching"? Why?

2. I remember a time when I faced a fear-filled trial and, like Peter, I began to sink as my faith was distracted by the waves of adversity. What ultimately made the difference in my growing faith was . . .

3. The one person who has taught me most about a persevering faith is . . .

The key characteristics of this person who so clearly demonstrated a growing faith in the midst of a storm of life are:

PRACTICAL APPLICATION

1. Memorize James 1:12: "Blessed is the man who perseveres under trial, because when he has stood the test, he will receive the crown of life that God has promised to those who love him."

2. This week, try to monitor your life and circle of influence to notice opportunities to be stretched and to grow in faith. Consciously and consistently allow the emotion of fear to be a reminder of a faith-growing opportunity.

3. Commit yourself to pray regularly for a growing faith and for supernatural strength and spiritual grace to persevere.

PRAYERFUL MEDITATION

1. FEAR NOT—We can have strength and courage when facing fear-stretching situations.

"Joshua said to them, 'Do not be afraid; do not be discouraged. Be strong and courageous.'"
—Joshua 10:25

2. FEAR NOT—Our hearts can be filled with faith and security when confronted with fearful challenges in life.

"His heart is secure, he will have no fear; in the end he will look in triumph on his foes."
—Psalm 112:8

3. FEAR NOT—Even when overwhelmed and tempted to quit, even when our faith is weak and tested beyond our strength, God will walk with us and not forsake us.

"The LORD himself goes before you and will be with you; he will never leave you nor forsake you. Do not be afraid; do not be discouraged."
—Deuteronomy 31:8

Notes:
[1] Lucado, Max. *The Eye of the Storm*. Dallas: Word Publishing, 1991: 200-201.

chapter

Hope in the Promises of God

"And now these three remain: faith, hope and love" (1 Corinthians 13:13). "Hope that is seen is no hope at all. Who hopes for what he already has?" (Romans 8:24).

Another essential priority in the process of learning to harness the power of fear is hope. There is no more bleak word in our language than *hopeless*. Without hope, fear invades the soul and leaves it in despair, and we give up and become victims. "Hope deferred makes the heart sick" (Proverbs 13:12). Hope is faith in the future tense, while faith (correctly translated as "courage") is the process of responding to a difficult situation by acting, doing, being, and behaving. Hope gives us the confidence we need to hang in there until we win. Hope fills us with confident expectation for a better tomorrow and makes the present trial merely a bumpy road. Hope spurs the athlete to train and increase his strength. Hope inspires the musician to perfect his performance. Hope enables us to face that surgery, invest that money and take those classes, because we believe the present risk and sacrifice are worth the outcome. Hope is never a self-generated pep rally that invigorates and excites us; rather, it is a hardy confidence to look beyond the here and now and glimpse a promising future. Martin Luther said that everything that is done in the world is done by hope.

Elpis, the New Testament word translated *hope*, means confident expectation. Because I possess a confident expectation I have the courage to do what I must in fearful circumstances. Hope is the confidence; faith is the courage. These two terms are at the core of any major accomplishment in life and are prerequisites to success in spiritual warfare. How do we generate, build on, or build up this confident expectation so that it will be a key contributor to the solutions to domination by fear?

In his book *When All Hell Breaks Loose*, Steven Lawson relates the following story which dramatically and precisely depicts the priority of hope:

> A couple of years ago, Anne and I were in Dallas seeing her parents. Anne's mom was there for a cancer checkup, having made remarkable progress. James and Andrew, my twin sons, were just little babies at the time.
>
> We were driving back from Dallas late at night after seeing her folks. We used to drive an old diesel station wagon that you could hear for miles around. That diesel engine clanked louder than a dozen loose golf balls in a clothes dryer.
>
> We were coming back on the interstate, somewhere between Texarkana and Little Rock. The boys were asleep. Anne was half asleep (she never goes to sleep when I'm driving).

We were out in the middle of nowhere on Interstate 30. It was so dark that night that you couldn't see two feet in front of you without the headlights. As we were driving along, all of a sudden I felt a loss of power. I thought maybe the engine had just missed a bit. I looked up in the rear-view mirror and there were clouds of smoke coming out of the back of our car. Well, if you know me and my familiarity with cars, you'd know how hopeless this was!

I said, "Sweetheart, look!" Anne turned around and looked at the trail of smoke behind us, as the car literally began to coast. Cruising up a hill, I began to think, What are we going to do? It's almost midnight. We have a diesel car. Nobody works on diesel cars. Do I pull over to the side and walk for help? But it'll be miles to the next stop. And if I left them stranded on the side of the road, will I come back and find that someone has taken them? Maybe I'll just take Anne and the boys. But the boys aren't even walking yet, and I don't know how far Anne and I can go carrying both of the kids. Or, maybe we'll just have to sit in the car and wait for someone to help us. Of course, we could wait until the Second Coming before somebody would help us. What would we do?

As we coasted up to the ridge, I said, "Sweetheart, I'm just going to have to pull over. We can't go any farther, and I don't know what we're going to do."

Then I looked up and saw a sight. I still can't believe the sight I saw. Just over the ridge, there was a large sign with one word on it. "Hope." And there was an arrow pointing off to the exit ramp. And I said, "Sweetheart, look, there's hope."

By this point we were barely rolling forward.

You could hear the knocking of metal against metal in the engine. We coasted to the top of the exit ramp.

Two signs were turned on. One was a Chevrolet dealership. It was the only one within 100 miles that worked on diesel cars. And right across the highway was the second lighted sign— a Holiday Inn. Those were the only lights on in town. I said, "Sweetheart, there's hope."

It was Hope, Arkansas.

Listen, when you're at the end of your rope, there's still hope. No matter how impossible the situation seems—no matter how dark the night— there's always hope.

You may be spewing smoke out the back end of your life and have lost all power to go on. You may be just coasting, barely rolling forward. I want you to know there's hope.

Are you at the end of your rope? Remember, there's hope. He will pull you through.[1]

Confidently Expect Success

The hope-filled person faces his task with confidence. A karate expert can break a brick with his bare hand because he approaches his task with the confident expectation that his hand will penetrate the brick. The football team that believes winning is possible never stops playing its best until the final whistle blows. However, without hope—confident expectation—the game is lost before the kickoff.

A sick person with hope has a better chance of a rapid recovery (his immediate task) than the person without hope. According to Norman Cousins, "The patient's hopes are the physician's secret weapon. They are the hidden ingredients in any prescription."

The shepherd boy David came before Goliath with hope in the name of the Lord, confident of the task before him (see 1 Samuel 17:45-46). When God assigns a task to us, we can claim the same hope that David experienced. We can echo the words of Paul, "I can do everything through him who gives me strength" (Philippians 4:13).

A hope-filled person is not defeated in times of hardship. Those who survived the concentration camps were the ones who never gave up hope. Victor Frankl, Professor of Psychiatry and Neurology at the University of Vienna, provides a contemporary illustration of the incredible power of hope. Dr. Frankl spent three terrible years in the concentration camp at Auschwitz and personally watched dozens of people die through brutality and hunger. He developed an existential form of psychotherapy referred to as logotherapy. He believes that the most important fact of life is purpose in life. A person with a purpose and hope can endure any pain. A statistical survey involving nearly 8,000 students at 48 colleges and universities conducted by social scientists indicated the importance of purpose and hope in the minds of young people today. In response to the question, "What is the most important question as you anticipate graduating?" Only 16 percent indicated the importance of money or materialism. Nearly 75 percent responded that finding purpose and meaning was the most critical question. Frankl refers to the absence of hope and purpose as "sickness of the soul." He noted in the concentration camps that those who had hope and purpose outlived those who had no hope.

It is safe to conclude that many millions of people who have serious emotional and mental disorders have in common a spirit of "hopelessness" that characterizes their lives.

Paul told the Roman Christians, who were being persecuted for their faith, that "suffering produces perseverance; perseverance, character; and character, hope. And hope does not disappoint us, because God has poured out his love into our hearts by the Holy Spirit, whom he has given us" (Romans 5:3-5).

Hope-filled people are faithful despite hardship. Shadrach, Meshach, and Abednego decided that being thrown into the fiery furnace was worth their being true to God—whether He delivered them or not (Daniel 3:16-18). They exemplified the advice of the Apostle Paul when he instructed Timothy to "endure hardness with us like a good soldier of Christ Jesus" (2 Timothy 2:3).

God, recognizing that one of the Adversary's greatest weapons is to create fear in us, has given us many hope-filled promises in His Word that match fear's aggression. He is our heavenly Father, and what parent wants his child to live in fear? Just as earthly parents often do, God assures us of victory by reminding us of what He has done in the past.

Remember What God Has Already Done

When you are going through a fear-filled experience and feel that your hope is as weak and shaky as a newborn foal, God—the great I AM, the Lord Jehovah, Savior, Shepherd, Provider—reminds you to trust Him, actively, responsibly, and routinely with today's fears because of yesterday's victories. The psalmist says that not only are we to remember God's goodness toward us but we should also "tell the next generation the praiseworthy deeds of the LORD, his power, and the wonders he has done" (Psalm 78:4).

When Israel forgot all the things God had done for them, "God's anger rose against them" (v. 31). The psalmist describes how God had "brought his people out [of Egypt] like a flock," leading "them like sheep through the desert," guiding "them safely, so they were unafraid" (Psalm 78:52-53). But Israel had a short memory. They forgot how God had insulated them from the plagues in Egypt, drowned their enemies in the Red Sea, led them through the desert with a cloud by day and a pillar of fire by night, quenched their thirst in the arid desert by causing water to gush out of rocks. Yet, "They willfully put God to the test by demanding the food they craved. They spoke against God, saying, 'Can God spread a table in the desert? When he struck the rock, water gushed out, and streams flowed abundantly. But can he also give us food? Can he supply meat for his people?'" (Psalm 78:18-20). And God did just that; He caused manna to drop from the sky so that the people had three meals a day.

Such faithful care should have provoked the people to trust in God with a courageous faith and confident hope. It should have challenged them to manage any future fears and anxious moments with a spontaneous and abundant hope. But it didn't. "They forgot what he had done, the wonders he had shown them" (verse 11). When they forgot what God had already done, fear rushed in to fill the vacancy left by faith's glaring absence, which in turn gave way to complaint and a nasty spirit of discontent. Finally, God had enough. "When God heard them, he was very angry; he rejected Israel completely" (v. 59). Their fear-blinded memory had led to their fear-fueled murmuring. Fear has the power to close our minds to all God has done for us.

God repeatedly told the Israelites, and continues to tell us, of His faithfulness. He knows that we are prone to forget Him. Once we disregard His unchanging promise to care for us today and tomorrow with the same fidelity He has shown in the past, unbelief and all its ugly children—including fear—take up residence in our trembling hearts. Then the Adversary can get hold of us and magnify our fears.

Tap into God's Power

We can realize true hope that will help us in times of fear when we tap into God's power, the mighty power that will bring us into "the inner sanctuary behind the curtain, where Jesus, who went before us, has entered on our behalf" (Hebrews 6:19-20).

Paul prayed that God's followers would know "the hope to which [God] has called you, the riches of his glorious inheritance in the saints, and his incomparably great power for us who believe." He goes on to explain: "That power is like the working of his mighty strength, which he exerted in Christ when he raised him from the dead and seated him at his right hand in the heavenly realms, far above all rule and authority, power and dominion, and every title that can be given" (Ephesians 1:18-21). This same power that raised Christ from the dead and will someday bring us to the eternal "sanctuary" is available right now to help us through times of fear here on earth.

As they met in the "upper room" to eat their last supper with Jesus, they could almost touch the tension in the air. In just a few weeks, they would realize one aspect of the resurrection power of God. But now they were entering their hour of desperation. All their human navigation systems were sending foreboding signals that could not be humanly reconciled. Jesus had often tried to prepare them for what was about to take place, but is there really any preparation for such a tragic loss?

As the events of the trial and crucifixion unfolded, many of His followers watched his agony; some heard Him say, "It is finished"; all were traumatized by the loss. Filled with fear and uncertainty, they could not reconcile the promise of His presence, peace, comfort, courage, wisdom, and joy, with His devastating death.

Then came the news! He's ALIVE! Mary Magdalene

and the other Mary listened intently as an angel admonished, "Do not be afraid, for I know that you are looking for Jesus, who was crucified. He is not here; he has risen, just as he said" (Matthew 28:5-6). Then Jesus Himself met them, and His first words to them were, "Do not be afraid" (Matthew 28:10). All of God's promises were now validated, forever insured by the resurrection power of Jesus Christ. Forty days later they received the Pentecostal power of the Holy Spirit. No more were they plagued with fear of what would happen to them. No longer would the Adversary overcome them with feelings of doubt and dread. They became people who turned the world upside down (Acts 17:6).

Tapping into this great power will help each of us to "throw off everything that hinders and . . . run with perseverance the race marked out for us" (Hebrews 12:1).

Since Jesus has power over death, we can be assured that He also has all power over the circumstances in our lives that threaten us. Talk about hope—confident expectation!

This hope, this anchor of our souls (Hebrews 6:19), builds a storehouse of strength that enables us to endure the fears of this life. The reason for our hope can be summarized in one Word—Jesus—risen and coming again so we will be forever with Him.

Let God Encourage Us

"May our LORD Jesus Christ himself and God our Father, who loved us and by his grace gave us eternal encouragement and good hope, encourage your hearts and strengthen you" (2 Thessalonians 2:16).

One of my favorite promises appears in Isaiah 41:10, "So do not fear, for I am with you; do not be dismayed, for I am your God. I will strengthen you and help you; I will uphold you with my righteous right hand." A few verses later, the echo rings out, "For I am the LORD, your God, who takes hold of your right hand and says to you, Do not fear; I will help you" (Isaiah 41:13). As we turn the pages to the New Testament we find the early Church repeating the promises God gave to His people: "Never will I leave you; never will I forsake you" (Hebrews 13:5; Deuteronomy 31:6); "So we say with confidence, 'The LORD is my helper; I will not be afraid. What can man do to me?'" (Hebrews 13:6; Psalm 118:6-7).

Several years ago, I was flying to a seminar in Chicago. I customarily leave my Bible out on the plane's tray table as I review my seminar notes. On this trip a middle-aged couple sat next to me. The lady, noticing the Bible, nudged me and asked, "Are you a pastor, priest, clergyman, or what?" Then she added, "Do you have any prayers for the ill?" When I asked what she meant, she explained that her husband, seated by window, was dying of cancer. In fact, their trip was a farewell to their family; then he would return home to die.

When she asked me to pray for her husband, I asked if they believed in the Bible. They replied that they did. For the next half hour I shared many verses from God's Word about death, suffering, hope, and eternity. They asked if I would occupy the middle seat and tell them more about God. It was not long before both of them asked Jesus Christ into their hearts. A couple of weeks later, I talked to the man on the phone. He admitted that he was somewhat afraid to die, but not with the dread that once gripped him. Now both he and his wife understood the reality of pain and loss in death and separation, but the impact was clearly softened by the glorious truth of eternal hope. He died a few days later, never to know fear again.

"Why are you downcast, O my soul? Why so disturbed within me? Put your hope in God, for I will yet praise him, my Savior and my God" (Psalm 42:11).

Hope and confidence in God's promises enables us to face fear with the expectation that God is our refuge and strength. We will confidently expect His presence and provision when facing fear-inducing life circumstances and changes.

There is a story about the great Paderewski that captures the essence of how hope and confidence can keep us from quitting. The concert hall was packed, and it was just a few minutes before the noted pianist was to take the stage. A small boy slipped away from his parents' care and made his way up to the stage. He sat down at the huge grand piano and began to play "Chopsticks." Red-faced ushers ran up the aisles toward the stage, intent upon unseating the child. Before they got there, however, Paderewski quickly put on his tuxedo jacket, walked on stage, put his arms around the boy and began to improvise an accompaniment to "Chopsticks," whispering to the boy, "Don't quit! Don't quit! Don't quit!" The crowd broke out in a spontaneous applause.

So many times when we are faced with fear-inducing circumstances that rob us of hope, we are tempted to quit. But the Holy Spirit of God puts His loving arms around us and keeps whispering in our heart this hope-generating encouragement, "Don't quit! Don't quit! Don't quit!"

PERSONAL EVALUATION

1. I need spiritual hope in my life right now because I feel concerned about . . .

I will believe Paul's claim that "I can do everything through him who gives me strength" (Philippians 4:13).

2. I remember another time when I needed God's strength and He was there for me. It was when . . .

3. Believing in God's great power, today I will put my hand in His and trust Him to be my helper. (Pray now, asking God to give you hope and to help you in that difficult situation you are faced with.)

PRACTICAL APPLICATION

1. Memorize Hebrews 11:1: "Now faith is being sure of what we hope for and certain of what we do not see."

2. Hope is looking to the future with confidence even though its content is unknown. List what you consider to be the three most important future issues and situations that will require you to have spiritual hope or confident expectation.

3. Plan to study the topic of hope for an entire month in your private devotional time. Use a topical Bible or your own Bible index and read 10 verses each day that have the word *hope* in them.

PRAYERFUL MEDITATION

1. FEAR NOT—Hope is the endurance we have because of God's truth.

> *"Blessed is he whose help is the God of Jacob, whose hope is in the LORD his God."*
> —Psalm 146:5

2. FEAR NOT—God encourages us through hope.

> *"May our LORD Jesus Christ himself and God our Father, who loved us and by his grace gave us eternal encouragement and good hope, encourage your hearts and strengthen you in every good deed and word."*
> —2 Thessalonians 2:16-17

3. FEAR NOT—Our joy and peace are not spoiled by fear-causing circumstances.

> *"May the God of hope fill you with all joy and peace as you trust in him, so that you may overflow with hope by the power of the Holy Spirit."*
> —Romans 15:13

Notes:
[1]   Lawson, Steven J. *When All Hell Breaks Loose.* Colorado Springs: NavPress Publishing Group, 1993: 153-4.

chapter

10

Develop
Perfect Love

A nd now these three remain: faith, hope and
love. But the greatest of these is love"
(1 Corinthians 13:13).

Jesus said that love is the summation of the law:
"'Love the Lord your God with all your heart and with
all your soul and with all your mind.' This is the first
and greatest commandment. And the second is like it:
'Love your neighbor as yourself.' All the Law and the
Prophets hang on these two commandments"
(Matthew 22:37- 40). And, "Perfect love," John tells us,
"drives out fear" (1 John 4:18). Although the context
of this particular verse deals with facing Christ at the
judgment seat (he who walks in love need not fear an
embarrassing unrewarded examination before Christ),
John also applies it to Christian living and Christian
experiences. Self-love, without extending that love to
others, can cultivate a cowardly lifestyle; but supernatural, selfless love cultivates courage. "Perfect love

drives out fear." But it is equally obvious that chronic fear crowds love out of our hearts. How do we get around this dilemma?

The Greek word John used that is translated *drives* in the New International Version (more graphically expressed in the King James version as *casts*) is not a gentle verb; it means to throw or hurl, to get rid of—as we do with our garbage or stones in the path of the lawn mower. Perfect love—acting on its own—violently thrusts fear out of our lives.

Perhaps this brief family illustration will highlight the power of love to cast out fear. My son Mark was in the second grade and had always enjoyed school. But he began to resist getting ready and going to school. It was quite surprising to us. It began to affect his sleep and initiated a major emotional battle for him and a practical battle for us to get him to school each day. We finally caught on that he was afraid of his teacher. We made an appointment with his teacher and discovered that he was a bit on the non-traditional side in how he dressed and in his demeanor. We made a decision to pray for Mr. Kolb each night as a family. We made an opportunity to tell him the Gospel message. As a family we bought him a book that clearly presented the Gospel and Mark gave it to him for a Christmas present just before the Christmas break. Mark's attitude changed dramatically as he began to love Mr. Kolb through Christ. Literally and dramatically Mark's fear disappeared, and his love for Mr. Kolb became a motivation to go to school. Mr. Kolb asked to meet with Marlene and me right after the Christmas break. He wanted us to be the first to know that, as a result of Mark's love, our prayers, and the book, he had accepted Christ as Savior over the break. He has stayed in touch with Mark and attended his high school graduation, again expressing his thanksgiving for a little boy's love. Love drives out fear. It was truly supernatural and a great example of this final priority for overcoming fear.

God Loved Us First

John says we should "love one another, for love comes from God . . . This is how God showed his love among us: He sent his one and only Son into the world that we might live through him. This is love: not that we loved God, but that he loved us and sent his Son as an atoning sacrifice for our sins" (1 John 4:7,9-10). "You see, at just the right time, when we were still powerless, Christ died for the ungodly. . . . God demonstrates his own love for us in this: While we were still sinners, Christ died for us" (Romans 5:6,8). God is our example of love. He loved us when we were unlovely.

Thus, John says, "Everyone who loves has been born of God and knows God. Whoever does not love does not know God, because God is love" (1 John 4:7-8). So, we reason, since we have been born of God and know God and love God, it should be easy to love others, and therefore, be free of fear. Sounds easy. But we all know it's not because, on the other hand, fear is also at the root of our unwillingness to love. We are afraid, fearful that our needs or our wants will not be met, so we build walls instead of bridges in relationships with those who have the potential to deprive us of what we want. "What causes fights and quarrels among you? Don't they come from your desires that battle within you? You want something but don't get it. You kill and covet, but you cannot have what you want. You quarrel and fight" (James 4:1-2). So a lack of love springs from fear, but it also leads to fear. Without God's help it becomes a hopeless cycle.

Romans 6 says that we can break that cycle through the blood of Christ because sin—and the Evil One—no longer have a hold on us. "We died to sin;

how can we live in it any longer?" (Romans 6:2). "Do not offer the parts of your body to sin, as instruments of wickedness. . . . For sin shall not be your master" (verses 13-14). "He sent his one and only Son into the world that we might live through him" (1 John 4:9). "That we might live through him" is the answer to conquering fear through love. God's steadfast, unfailing, unconditional love holds us.

God Still Loves Us Today

While we are bound to Earth we need not be afraid of anyone or anything because of God's steadfast love. We will not fear going hungry or thirsty because God, our loving heavenly Father, who feeds the birds is even more concerned with providing for us (Matthew 6:25-26). We will not fear evil men or the Evil One because the "Lord is the stronghold of my life—of whom shall I be afraid? When evil men advance against me . . . they will stumble and fall" (Psalm 27:1-2).

We will not fear terrorists or being overpowered by foreign nations. "You may say to yourselves, 'These nations are stronger than we are' . . . But do not be afraid of them" (Deuteronomy 7:17-18). "I will not fear the tens of thousands drawn up against me on every side" (Psalm 3:6).

We will not fear physical harm because God either keeps us from harm or equips us to deal with it through His strength. All of this because "out of his glorious riches he may strengthen you with power through his Spirit in your inner being, so that Christ may dwell in your hearts through faith . . . .[so that you] being rooted and established in love, may have power . . . to grasp how wide and long and high and deep is the love of Christ, and to know this love that surpasses knowledge—that you may be filled to the measure of all the fullness of God" (Ephesians 3:16-19).

We can safely hide under the cover of God's protective wings (Psalm 91:4); His loving presence never leaves us (Matthew 28:20). Whenever we forget how the Lord loves and cuddles us, we should read Psalm 103. It reminds us of His tender mercies, loving-kindness, graciousness, healing, forgiveness; "He satisfies my desires with good things" (verse 5). Verse 4 reminds us that the primary evidence of God's love is that He has redeemed our lives from destruction. This redemption, the ultimate demonstration of God's perfect love toward us, required the ultimate sacrifice, Christ's death (Romans 5:8; 1 John 4:9-10).

Because we are redeemed, we can live in the midst of God's love (1 John 4:16). From the vantage point of this security, we can rejoice in the truth of His love and say with the psalmist, "The Lord is with me; I will not be afraid. What can man do to me?" (Psalm 118:6). "We are more than conquerors through him who loved us. For I am convinced that neither death nor life, neither angels nor demons, neither the present nor the future, nor any powers, neither height nor depth, nor anything else in all creation, will be able to separate us from the love of God that is in Christ Jesus our Lord" (Romans 8:37-39). Rejoicing in this truth frees us to love those whom we might otherwise have reason to fear.

God is not just the source of love; He *is* love (1 John 4:16). To know God is to embrace ultimate love. Because this truth is so all-encompassing, it is the first truth taught in the little tots' Sunday school. We may take it for granted, like the air we breathe. But this foundational truth is worthy of celebration. Let's rejoice in God's love.

God Will Always Love Us

Love also cares about the long-range program. Often we question things that happen in our lives or

in the lives of others that seem harsh and unloving.
We ask God, as Job did, "Why have you made me
your target? Have I become a burden to you?" (Job
7:20). Or, "If I have sinned, what have I done to you,
O watcher of men?" God, in the context of His bound-
less love, tends to the details of our daily lives, even
keeping track of the number of hairs on our heads.
But He never loses sight of His greater plan, that life-
long—and eternal—program for our benefit and His
glory. We are His beloved children, and "the Lord dis-
ciplines those he loves" (Hebrews 12:6), which could
include hardship, because He is training us for holy
living and purity.

The author of Hebrews explains that God lets us
go through some painful, even fearful times out of
love, as a form of discipline, so that we can be made
stronger. "Later on . . . it produces a harvest of righteousness and peace for those who have been trained
by it" (Hebrews 12:11). Many who lost their loved
ones—mothers, fathers, and little children—in the
Oklahoma City bombing expressed this belief as they
said on national TV, "I know something good will
come from this!" In the midst of their grief and pain
they were able to look to a heavenly Father—who
had once watched His own Son being killed—and to
know His intense, all-wise, steadfast love.

Sometimes God uses other people in this process.
For example, when Joseph's brothers sold him as a
slave to the Egyptians, they did not realize that they
were part of a master plan which eventually benefit-
ted Joseph, his entire family, and the whole nation of
Israel. But Joseph rejoiced in the truth of God's sovereign care and could later say to his brothers, "Do not
be distressed and do not be angry with yourselves for
selling me here, because it was to save lives that God
sent me ahead of you . . . to preserve for you a rem-
nant on earth and to save your lives by a great deliv-

erance" (Genesis 45:5,7). Rejoicing in this truth freed Joseph to love his brothers.

Richard Nixon faced the humiliation and pain of public demise as a result of the Watergate scandal. All of his life he had served and loved the country that he failed, and he could not cope with the realization. In his book, *In The Arena*, Mr. Nixon tells a story of how his hopelessness and despair were banished through a simple act of authentic and divinely timed expression of love.

> When I woke up again, I asked Pat to come in. I now knew that I was in pretty desperate shape. Throughout the time we have known each other, Pat and I have seldom revealed our physical disabilities to each other. This time, I couldn't help it. I said that I didn't think I was going to make it. She gripped my hand and said almost fiercely, "Don't talk that way. You have got to make it. You must not give up." . . . Shortly afterwards, a nurse came in and wheeled me into another room with a window. She pointed to a small plane with a sign trailing behind that read: "God loves you and so do we." I learned later that Ruth Graham and some of her friends had arranged it. I am convinced now that had it not been for the support of my family and the thoughts and prayers of countless numbers of people I have never met and that I would never have a chance to thank, I would not have made it."[1]

Love! That's the essence of God's nature, the summation of the law and the prophets, our highest motivation with powerful healing potential. Its absence begets guilt and fear. The more we know of God, the more we are able to love. In knowing and experiencing this love, we have love to return to Him and to others.

The Most Excellent Way

How do you score in the love department of your life? Paul calls love "the most excellent way" in 1 Corinthians 13. Then he goes on to list love's ingredients: Love is patient, kind, protective, trusting, hopeful, and persevering. Love is not envious, boastful, proud, rude, self-seeking, or easily angered. Love does not keep record of wrongs, nor does it delight in evil. Love never fails. Supernatural, Biblical, selfless love is absolutely trustworthy. You can count it true!

"Love is patient," Paul says. He told the Galatians that patience is one fruit of the Spirit (5:22). Then in Ephesians he tells us to "be patient, bearing with one another in love" (4:2). In other words, we have to work at it. Love-motivated patience develops slowly, one victory after another, until we know how to love ultimately.

"Love is kind." Unkindness is often fear-motivated or fear-related. Love does not try to wound another with harmful deeds or destructive speech. "Do not let any unwholesome talk come out of your mouths, but only what is helpful for building others up according to their needs. . . . Be kind and compassionate to one another" (Ephesians 4:29, 32). In this passage Paul does not say "try" to do these things, but rather "do not let" and "be kind"; these are commandments. "I can do everything through him who gives me strength"; I can be kind—even if others are rude; I can guard my tongue, grit my teeth, measure my words, and be kind and compassionate.

"Love does not delight in evil but rejoices with the truth" (1 Corinthians 13:6). The "truth" we rejoice in is God's truth. Hebrews 6:18 tells us that it is impossible for God to lie. Therefore, we know His word is true. As we continue to find joy in His truth, His Spirit works in our lives. Then the miracle of love begins—

without our trying to force its growth. One by one, our fears are engulfed by love. The miracle begins with finding joy, peace, and power in the Word of God.

The next few ingredients of love are: love "does not envy, it does not boast, it is not proud. It is not rude, it is not self-seeking, it is not easily angered, it keeps no record of wrongs" (1 Corinthians 13:4-5). Paul says that being aware of the fact that you are pretty good at loving would tend to cause you to puff up with pride, and love again would be lost.

Perfect love "always protects, always trusts, always hopes, always perseveres. Love never fails" (verses 7-8). When we see others as fellow heirs of the grace of God, a miracle begins to happen: love flourishes and fear wilts. Perfect love drives out fear.

We cannot learn "the most excellent way" in one day. But we begin by embracing the Love which God sent to us—the Lord Jesus Christ. Then we start to live as Christ lived. Little by little we will embrace love's ingredients until we know how perfect love can toss fear out of our lives.

Eric and Janet Jeffery, a couple in their seventies, decided to roll up their sleeves and do something about today's troubled teens. When they entered the high school classrooms as volunteer tutors, culture shock had them shivering with apprehension, but they put aside cowardly fear and determined to extend love to troubled youth despite feelings of fear. What started with two now numbers 50! As a direct result of their stepping out to demonstrate the love of Christ to at-risk high school students, every public school in Escondido, California, now requests tutors from the Jefferys' group of senior citizens. More than 75 students have elected to attend a Christian summer camp, and 25 have come to know the Lord. What a powerful love! This unique ministry could easily have been short-circuited by fear.

Remember we began this book with an emphasis on spiritual warfare and Satan's evil schemes. Now we conclude with an encouraging reminder of God's truth. "Stand firm then, with the belt of truth [the source of your rejoicing] buckled around your waist, with the breastplate of righteousness in place, and with your feet fitted with the readiness that comes from the gospel in peace. In addition to all this, take up the shield of faith, with which you can extinguish all the flaming arrows" and you will take no risk. Holding the "sword of the Spirit, which is the word of God" (Ephesians 6:14-17), frees you to nullify fear as you reach out in love not only to your "brothers" but also to your enemies.

The story is told of a man visiting hell who entered a banquet hall replete with long tables and pots of delicious-smelling stew awaiting the guests. He watched as one guest after another sat down and reached for a spoon. Each one became frustrated as he discovered that the spoon handles were longer than his arms. Throughout all eternity, none of them would ever manage to get a spoonful of the tempting food into his mouth. The visitor then toured heaven. He thought that he was in the same banquet hall. But there was a big difference. The guests at the heavenly tables were using the long-handled spoons to feed each other.

The miracle of perfect love can never happen unless we first personally experience God's love by accepting that forgiveness from the One who has the power to forgive because His Son, Jesus Christ, died for those sins and rose again. Next, because we have experienced God's forgiveness, we are free from the power that causes us to fear, and we can go to the next step of ridding our lives of destructive, manipulative fear.

God bestows three divine treasures—"faith, hope, love. But the greatest of these is love" (1 Corinthians

13:13). Faith conquers fear, hope gives the endurance necessary to withstand fear, and love tosses out the remnants of any fear that is left. All three are essential in the battle against the bondage of fear, and all three are built into our lives by the same means—knowing, believing, and applying the Word of God.

Attain Lasting Solutions: One Step at a Time

During the construction of the Alaska oil pipeline, seven oil company officials were flying to a remote site to do some studies on the geography. Quite unexpectedly a major blizzard came up. The plane was forced to make an emergency landing. The plane crashed, destroying the communication system. News headlines reported the crash and suggested that the men did not survive. The company summoned the victims' families from the mainland to await rescue attempts. Searchers finally gave up after nearly seven days.

Ten days after the crash the men showed up at a small Alaskan village. They all suffered from injuries as a result of the crash and were frost bitten, but they had walked nearly 300 miles to the village. The press asked, "How is it possible that you walked nearly 300 miles through some of the most unforgiving terrain in the dead of winter?"

The leader of the men slowly and deliberately cleared his throat. Then he quietly responded, "Oh, we didn't walk 300 miles. You see, we walked one mile—300 times."

That's it! When we think of harnessing fear and developing faith, it seems like a 300-mile journey. There is so much involved. But we can take one step at a time, little by little.

PERSONAL EVALUATION

1. Which of the specific characteristic traits of Biblical love is the most mature in my Christian experience?

2. Which of the specific characteristic traits of Biblical love needs the most attention in terms of pursuing growth and maturity?

3. In what ways do I daily experience and express Biblical love?

PRACTICAL APPLICATION

1. Memorize 1 John 4:18: "There is no fear in love. But perfect love drives out fear, because fear has to do with punishment. The man who fears is not made perfect in love."

2. What one person in your circle of influence best illustrates Biblical love? List three specific characteristics of this person that can be found in 1 Corinthians 13.

3. Using a topical Bible, study 10 verses each week that include the word *love* in them. Ask God to help you cultivate a growing selfless, sensitive love for others.

PRAYERFUL MEDITATION

1. FEAR NOT—I have experienced God's steadfast love; therefore I can, in turn, express love to others.

"For God did not give us a spirit of timidity, but a spirit of power, of love and of self-discipline."
—II Tim. 1:7

2. FEAR NOT—God's love keeps me safe in His holy arms.

"The LORD is my light and my salvation—whom shall I fear? The LORD is the stronghold of my life— of whom shall I be afraid?"
—Psalm 27:1-2

3. FEAR NOT—God's love is personal and He holds us in His protective care.

"Indeed, the very hairs of your head are all numbered. Don't be afraid; you are worth more than many sparrows."
—Luke 12:7

Notes:
1. Nixon, Richard. *In the Arena*. New York: Simon and Schuster, 1990: 23-4.